FOREIGN AID: CONTROL, CORRUPT, CONTAIN?

FOREIGN AID: CONTROL, CORRUPT, CONTAIN?

ANDREW A. BEALINGER
EDITOR

Novinka Books
An imprint of Nova Science Publishers, Inc.
New York

Library of Congress Cataloging-in-Publication Data:
Available Upon Request

ISBN: 1-60021-067-8

Published by Nova Science Publishers, Inc. ✤
New York

CONTENTS

PREFACE

Foreign aid has long become a misnomer. It might properly be called 'foreign policy with funds.' Foreign aid packages have become tools to help rein in countries who disagree with this or that foreign policy, to allow leaders of those receiving countries to become privately wealthy and thus beholden to the donor country, and to stipulate that up to 40% of the total 'aid' must be in the form of contracts to companies from the donor country who are often politically tied to the political administration of the donor country. This new book provides the background information on important aspects of foreign aid.

The report presented in chapter 1 provides an overview of the U.S. foreign aid program, by addressing a number of the more frequently asked questions regarding the subject.

Chapter 2 focuses on the U.S. Department of Agriculture (USDA) which forecasted that FY2004 agricultural exports would be a record $61.5 billion, exceeding the FY1996 record of $59.8 billion. Projected imports of $51.5 billion, also a record, would result in an export surplus of $10 billion, $500 million less than in 2003. This chapter goes on in detail as to how USDA operates four kinds of export and food aid programs that are authorized in the 2002 farm bill (P.L. 107-171), in the Farm Security and Rural Investment Act (FSRIA), and in permanent legislation. These programs include direct export subsidies, export promotion, export credit guarantees, and foreign food aid. Legislative authority for most of these programs now extends to the end of 2007. Export subsidies, but not other U.S. export and food aid programs, are subject to reduction commitments agreed to in multilateral trade negotiations.

Chapter 3 discusses a growing question raised by some Members of Congress concerns the level of funding to support MCC programs. Some, noting that proposals received by the Corporation in 2004 totaled more than $4.2 billion, fear that insufficient funds might force the MCC to reduce the number of recipients or the size of the grants. Others, however, believe that the slower-than-anticipated pace of Compact agreements means that the Corporation has or will have enough resources, and support reductions to the $3 billion FY2006 request. The Foreign Operations Appropriations, as passed the House (H.R. 3057), recommends $1.75 billion for MCC programs next year, while the Senate Appropriations Committee proposes $1.8 billion (also H.R. 3057).

The United States is the world's major provider of international food aid to low-income developing countries. The report presented in chapter 4 provides three indicators of the U.S. contribution to global food aid: (1) shipments of major donors compiled by the International Grains Council, (2) U.S. contributions to the United Nations World Food Program (WFP), and (3) the U.S. commitment under the Food Aid Convention (FAC).

U.S. food aid accounted for 59% of food aid shipments by major donors during 1995-2003. A substantial portion of U.S. food aid is channeled through the WFP. During 1996-2004, around 48% of the food aid distributed by the WFP came from the United States. The Food Aid Convention (FAC), now expired, was an agreement among donor countries to provide a minimum amount of food aid to low-income developing countries. The food aid commitment by all FAC signatories was approximately 4.9 million metric tons (mmt). The United States pledged to provide 2.5 mmt or 51% of the total commitment.

In: Foreign Aid: Control, Corrupt, Contain?   ISBN 1-60021-067-8
Editor: A. A. Bealinger, pp. 1-40   © 2006 Nova Science Publishers, Inc.

Chapter 1

FOREIGN AID: AN INTRODUCTORY OVERVIEW OF U.S. PROGRAMS AND POLICY[*]

Curt Tarnoff[1] and Larry Nowels[2]

ABSTRACT

Foreign assistance is a fundamental component of the international affairs budget and is viewed by many as an essential instrument of U.S. foreign policy. Since the end of the Cold War, many have proposed significant changes in the size, composition, and purpose of the program, several of which have been adopted. The focus of U.S. foreign aid policy has also been transformed since the terrorist attacks of September 11, 2001. This report provides an overview of the U.S. foreign aid program, by addressing a number of the more frequently asked questions regarding the subject.

There are five major categories of foreign assistance: bilateral development aid, economic assistance supporting U.S. political and security goals, humanitarian aid, multilateral economic contributions, and military aid. Due largely to the recent implementation two new foreign aid initiatives — the Millennium Challenge Corporation and the Global AIDS Initiative — bilateral development assistance has become the largest category of U.S. aid.

---

[*] Excerpted from CRS Report 98-916, dated April 15, 2004.

In 2004, the United States is providing some form of foreign assistance to about 150 countries. Israel and Egypt continue, as they have since the late 1970s, as the largest recipients, although Iraq, receiving over $20 billion for reconstruction activities since mid-2003, is the biggest recipient in FY2004. The importance of Latin America counter-narcotics efforts is also evident, with Bolivia, Peru, and more recently, Colombia, among the top U.S. aid recipients. The impact of the terrorist attacks on September 11, 2001, and the subsequent use of foreign aid to support the war on terrorism is clearly seen in the country-aid allocations for FY2004. Afghanistan, Pakistan, Turkey, Jordan, and Indonesia are key partners in the war on terrorism.

By nearly all measures, the amount of foreign aid provided by the United States declined for several decades but has grown in the past few years. After hitting an all-time low in the mid1990s, total foreign assistance (but excluding Iraq reconstruction) for FY2003/2004, in real terms, has been larger than any two-year period since the mid-1980s. The 0.2% of U.S. gross national product represented by foreign aid obligations the past two years, however, is among the smallest amounts in the last half-century. The United States is the largest international economic aid donor in dollar terms but is the smallest contributor among the major donor governments when calculated as a percent of gross national income.

The U.S. Agency for International Development (USAID) manages the bulk of bilateral economic assistance; the Treasury Department handles most multilateral aid; and the Department of Defense (DOD) and the State Department administer military and other security-related programs. The Millennium Challenge Corporation is a new foreign aid agency created in 2004. The House International Relations and Senate Foreign Relations Committees have primary congressional responsibility for authorizing foreign aid programs while the House and Senate Appropriations Foreign Operations Subcommittees manage bills appropriating most foreign assistance funds.

INTRODUCTION

U.S. foreign aid is a fundamental component of the international affairs budget and is viewed by many as an essential instrument of U.S. foreign policy.[1] Each year, it is the subject of extensive congressional debate and legislative initiatives. Since the end of the Cold War, many have proposed significant changes in the size, composition, and purpose of the program, several of which have been adopted. The focus of U.S. foreign aid policy has also been transformed since the terrorist attacks of September 11, 2001.

This report, generally using a question-and-answer format, addresses a number of the more frequently asked queries regarding the U.S. foreign aid program, its objectives, costs, organization, the role of Congress, and how it compares to those of other aid donors. In particular, the discussion attempts to not only present a current "snap-shot" of American foreign assistance, but also to illustrate the extent to which this instrument of U.S. foreign policy has changed from past practices, especially since the end of the Cold War and during the period following September 11, 2001.

Data presented in the report are the most current, reliable figures available, usually covering the period through FY2004 or, where possible, the most recent year. Dollar amounts are drawn from a variety of sources, including the Office of Management and Budget (OMB), U.S. Agency for International Development (USAID), and from annual Foreign Operations and other appropriations acts. As new data become obtainable or additional issues and questions arise, the report will be modified and revised.

FOREIGN AID GOALS AND PROGRAMS

What are the Goals and Objectives of U.S. Foreign Assistance?

Foreign assistance supports a great many objectives. Especially since the September 11 terrorist attacks in the United States, foreign aid has taken on a more strategic sense of importance, cast frequently in terms of contributing to the global war on terrorism. In September 2002, President Bush released his Administration's National Security Strategy that established global development, for the first time, as the third "pillar" of U.S. national security, along with defense and diplomacy. Also in 2002, executive branch foreign assistance budget justifications began to underscore the war on terrorism as the top foreign aid priority, highlighting amounts of U.S. assistance to about 30 "front-line" states in the terrorism war. The substantial reconstruction programs in Afghanistan and Iraq — which total more in FY2004 than the combined budgets of all other aid programs — are also part of the emphasis on using foreign aid to combat terrorism.

At roughly the same time that fighting terrorism became the leading concern of American foreign aid, the Bush Administration announced other significant initiatives that have defined and strengthened two additional key foreign assistance goals: promoting economic growth and reducing poverty, and combating the global HIV/AIDS pandemic. The Millennium Challenge

Corporation (MCC) is a new aid delivery concept, established in early 2004, that is intended to concentrate significantly higher amounts of U.S. resources in a few low- and low-middle income countries that have demonstrated a strong commitment to political, economic, and social reforms. If fully funded, $5 billion will be available by FY2006 to support these "best development performers" in order to accelerate economic growth and lower the number of people living in absolute poverty.

Addressing global health problems has further become a core U.S. aid objective in recent years. Congress created a separate appropriation account for Child Survival and Health activities in the mid-1990s and increased funding for international HIV/AIDS and other infectious disease programs. President Bush's announcement at his 2003 State of the Union message of a five-year, $15 billion effort to combat AIDS, malaria, and tuberculosis has added greater emphasis to this primary foreign assistance objective.

Beyond these recently emerging foreign aid goals, other prominent objectives that have continued since the early 1990s have included supporting peace in the Middle East through assistance to Israel, Egypt, Jordan, and the Palestinians; fostering democratization and stability for countries in crisis, such as Bosnia, Haiti, Rwanda, Kosovo, and Liberia; facilitating democratization and free market economies in Central Europe and the former Soviet Union; suppressing international narcotics production and trafficking through assistance to Colombia and other Andean drug-producing countries; and alleviating famine and mitigating refugee situations in places throughout the world.

Arguably, from the end of World War II until the early 1990s, the underlying rationale for providing foreign aid was the same as that for all U.S. foreign policy - the defeat of communism. U.S. aid programs were designed to promote economic development and policy reforms, in large part to create stability and reduce the attraction to communist ideology and to block Soviet diplomatic links and military advances. The programs also supported other U.S. policy goals, such as reducing high rates of population growth, promoting wider access to health care, and expanding the availability of basic education in the developing world, advancing U.S. trade interests, and protecting the environment. If these secondary goals were also achieved, U.S. aid programs could be promoted as delivering "more bang for the buck". With the end of the Cold War, no consensus emerged over what should be the new overarching rationale for U.S. aid programs. Consequently, many of these secondary objectives of foreign assistance are more vulnerable to challenge. Some may ultimately be discarded, while others are being incorporated into new initiatives, representing some of the emerging foreign aid priorities noted above.

The Clinton Administration emphasized the promotion of "sustainable development" as the new, post-Cold War main strategy of those parts of the foreign aid program under the aegis of the U.S. Agency for International Development (USAID). Economic assistance supported six inter-related goals: achievement of broad-based, economic growth; development of democratic systems; stabilization of world population and protection of human health, sustainable management of the environment; building human capacity through education and training; and meeting humanitarian needs.

Early in the Bush Administration these goals were modified around three "strategic pillars"of 1) economic growth, agriculture, and trade; 2) global health; and 3) democracy, conflict prevention, and humanitarian assistance. More recently, a USAID White Paper on American foreign aid identified five "core" operational goals of U.S. foreign assistance:

- Promoting transformational development, especially in the areas of governance, institutional capacity, and economic restructuring;
- Strengthening fragile states;
- Providing humanitarian assistance
- Supporting U.S. geostrategic interests, particularly in countries such as Iraq, Afghanistan, Pakistan, Jordan, Egypt, and Israel; and
- Mitigating global and international ills, including HIV/AIDS.[2]

Generally speaking, different types of foreign aid support different objectives. Focusing on any single element of the aid program would produce a different sense of the priority of any particular U.S. objective. But there is also considerable overlap between categories of aid. Multilateral aid serves many of the same objectives as bilateral development assistance, although through different channels. International financial institutions have become the predominant players in Central Europe and the former Soviet Union, serving U.S. economic and security objectives in those regions. Both military assistance and economic security assistance serve U.S. objectives in the Middle East and South Asia. Drug interdiction activities, backed in some cases with military assistance and alternative development programs, are integrated elements of American counter-narcotics efforts in the Andean region and elsewhere.

Iraq Reconstruction Funding

The U.S. assistance program to Iraq — the largest aid initiative since the 1948-1951 Marshall Plan — supports the long-term reconstruction requirements of the country following the March 2003 U.S. invasion and overthrow of the regime of Saddam Hussein. Funds have been mostly directed at improving the security capabilities of the Iraqi police and armed forces, at making rapid improvements in infrastructure — including electricity, oil, water and sewage, and telecommunications — and promoting democratization efforts. To date, two emergency supplemental appropriations have provided funds for these purposes (P.L. 108-11 for FY2003 and P.L. 108-106 for FY2004). The bulk of Iraq assistance — nearly $21 billion of the $23.7 billion that is expected to support the program — is held in an Iraq Relief and Reconstruction Fund controlled by the Office of the President and delegated to other executive branch agencies.

Because of the size of the Iraq reconstruction effort, including funding figures in FY2003 and FY2004 totals tends to overshadow and obscure key trends in changing foreign aid budget and policy priorities. Therefore, unless otherwise noted in the text and figures, funding amounts noted in this report exclude figures for Iraq reconstruction. In many instances, however, a notation is made stating what a particular amount would equal if Iraq assistance was included.

What are the Different Types of Foreign Aid?

Although there are many ways to group foreign aid by types of assistance, this report organizes programs into five major categories, illustrated in Figure 1 below.

Bilateral Development Assistance

Development assistance programs are designed chiefly to foster sustainable broad-based economic progress and social stability in developing countries. For FY2004, Congress appropriated $6.2 billion in such assistance, an amount accounting for 30% of total foreign aid appropriations. Most of these funds are managed by the U.S. Agency for International Development (USAID) and are used for long-term projects in the areas of economic reform and private sector development, democracy promotion, environmental protection, population and human health. Development activities gaining more prominence in recent years have been debt relief for the poorest nations, mostly in Africa, and support for treatment of HIV/AIDS and other diseases. (See question on sectoral priorities below.) Other bilateral development assistance goes to distinct institutions, such as the Peace Corps, the Inter-American Development Foundation, the African Development Foundation, the Trade and Development Agency, and the new Millenium Challenge Corporation. The latter is expected to provide significant levels of assistance to countries that meet specific standards of good governance and free market economic reform.

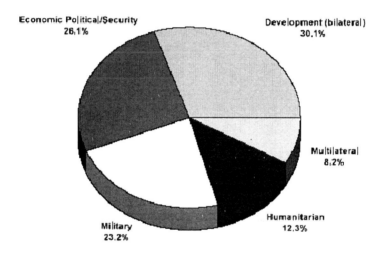

Figure 1. Aid Program Composition — FY2004

Economic Aid Supporting U.S. Political and Security Objectives

In FY2004, Congress appropriated $5.4 billion, 26% of total assistance, for five major programs whose primary purpose is to meet special U.S. economic, political, or security interests. The bulk of these funds — $3 billion — are provided through the Economic Support Fund (ESF), an aid category designed to advance American strategic goals with economic assistance. Since the 1979 Camp David accords and especially since the end of the Cold War, most ESF has gone to support the Middle East Peace Process. Since 9/11, much ESF has targeted countries of importance in the war on terrorism. ESF funds can be used for development projects (about

57% of the total in FY2004), or in other ways, such as cash transfers, to help countries stabilize their economies and service foreign debt (about 43% in FY2004).

With the demise of the Soviet empire, the United States established two new aid programs which met particular strategic political interests. The SEED (Support for East European Democracy Act of 1989) and the FREEDOM Support Act (Freedom for Russia and Emerging Eurasian Democracies and Open Markets Support Act of 1992) programs were designed to help Central Europe and the new independent states of the former Soviet Union (NIS) achieve democratic systems and free market economies. In FY2004, SEED countries are allocated $442.4 million while the NIS receives $583.5 million in appropriated funds.

Several other global issues that are considered threats to U.S. security and well-being — terrorism, narcotics, crime and weapons proliferation — have received special attention from the foreign assistance program, especially since the war on terror began. Each of these programs provide a range of law enforcement activities, training, and equipment. In FY2004, the anti-narcotics and crime program (excluding alternative development activities) accounts for about $900 million in foreign aid appropriations — over half of which is for an Andean anti-narcotics initiative. Anti-terrorism programs add another $146.4 million, and weapons proliferation-related activities are funded at $250 million.

Humanitarian Assistance

In FY2004, Congress appropriated $2.55 billion, 12% of assistance, for programs of humanitarian aid.[3] Unlike, development assistance programs, which are often viewed as long-term efforts that may have the effect of preventing future crises from developing, three programs are devoted largely to the immediate alleviation of humanitarian emergencies. The bulk of humanitarian assistance goes to the refugee program administered by the State Department. It supports, with about $785.5 million in FY2004, a number of refugee relief organizations, including the U.N. High Commission for Refugees and the International Committee of the Red Cross. The Offices of Foreign Disaster Assistance (OFDA) and Transition Initiatives (OTI) in USAID provide relief, rehabilitation, and reconstruction assistance to victims of manmade and natural disasters, activities totaling $529 million in FY2004.

Supplementing both programs is food assistance (about $1.2 billion in FY2004). The food aid program, generically referred to as P.L. 480 or the Food for Peace program, provides U.S. agricultural commodities to developing countries. USAID-administered Title II grant food aid is mostly provided for humanitarian relief but may also be used for development-oriented purposes by private voluntary organizations (PVOs) or through multilateral organizations, such as the World Food Program. Title II funds are also used to support the "farmer-to-farmer" program which sends hundreds of U.S. volunteers to provide technical advice and training to farm and food-related groups throughout the world. A new program begun in 2002, the McGovern-Dole International Food for Education and Child Nutrition Program, provides commodities, technical assistance, and finance for school feeding and child nutrition programs ($50 million in FY2004).[4]

Multilateral Assistance

A relatively small share of U.S. foreign assistance — 8% in FY2004 — is combined with contributions from other donor nations to finance multilateral development projects. For FY2004, Congress appropriated $1.7 billion for such activities implemented by international organizations, like the United Nations Children's Fund (UNICEF) and the United Nations Development Program (UNDP), and by multilateral development banks (MDBs), such as the World Bank. On average, U.S. contributions represent about 20% of total donor transfers to the MDBs.

Military Assistance

The United States provides military assistance to U.S. friends and allies to help them acquire U.S. military equipment and training. Congress appropriated $4.8 billion for military assistance in FY2004, 23% of total U.S. foreign aid. There are three main programs. Foreign Military Financing (FMF), $4.6 billion in FY2004, is a grant program that enables governments to receive equipment from the U.S. government or to access equipment directly through U.S. commercial channels. Like ESF, most FMF grants support the security needs of Israel and Egypt. The International Military Education and Training program (IMET), $91 million, offers military training on a grant basis to foreign military officers and personnel. Peacekeeping funds ($124.5 million in FY2004, are used to support voluntary non-U.N. operations and training for an African crisis response force and for the Afghanistan National Army.

As Figure 2 indicates, there have been some gradual shifts in program emphasis during the past 15 years. Military assistance as a share of total aid obligations continued declining through FY2004, a trend that began after military aid peaked in FY1984 at 42%. In FY1996-97, it rebounded from 24.8% to about a 30% share, not because military assistance grew in absolute terms, but because other categories of foreign aid fell significantly while military grants, especially for Israel and Egypt, remained constant. The proportion of aid represented by military programs declined further in FY1999 to roughly 23%, mainly due to the "graduation" of Greece and Turkey as military aid recipients. Military assistance rose again in FY2000 (to 30%) largely because of a one-time Middle East peace supplemental for Israel and Jordan. After falling back to about one-fourth of total U.S. foreign aid, military assistance jumped to over 28% in FY2003 as the United States provided additional security support to many of the front-line states in the war on terrorism and other countries that might faces new external threats due to the pending conflict in Iraq. By FY2004, its share fell to 23.2%, the lowest proportion of the period, largely due to the rise in prominence of the development assistance category.

Economic strategic and political aid has remained fairly stable over the past 15 years, spiking in FY1993 with the growth of programs in the former Soviet Union. Funding for a Middle East peace supplemental, the Andean Counter-narcotics Initiative and economic support for countries assisting U.S. efforts in the war on terrorism pushed strategic-oriented economic aid above a 30% share between FY2000 and FY2003. The proportion of foreign aid appropriated for this grouping dropped to 26% in FY2004, reflecting somewhat the impact of a continuing ten-year plan to reduce economic aid to Israel and Egypt, and, except in the case of Afghanistan, less robust aid for "front-line" states in the war on terrorism.

Perhaps the most striking trend in this period has been the growth in development-related assistance, including humanitarian, food aid and contributions to multilateral institutions. Development-related aid rose steadily from a 38% share in FY1990 to nearly 49% by FY1994. The growth of more politically-driven economic programs in Central Europe and the former Soviet Union, plus sizable cuts to development aid in FY1996/1997 and increased emphasis on security assistance following the September 11 terrorist attacks, drove the share of its allocation down to an average of 42% during the late 1990s through FY2003. With the approval of significant amounts of funding for two new presidential aid priorities, the Millennium

Challenge Corporation and the Global AIDS Initiative, development assistance grew to represent over half of total foreign aid in FY2004, the highest level during the past 15 years.

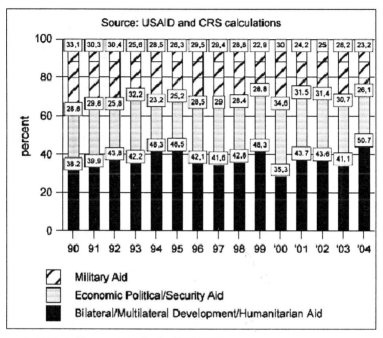

Figure 2. Shifts in Program Emphasis, 1990-2004

What are the Funding Priorities of Bilateral Economic Assistance?

The largest component of U.S. foreign aid finances bilateral economic assistance programs managed directly by USAID, or in some cases jointly by USAID and the State Department. This cluster of assistance roughly matches the combined two categories of bilateral development aid and economic political/security programs illustrated in Figure 1, above, that are managed by USAID and the Department of State.[5] Congress appropriates funds for these activities in seven accounts included in annual Foreign Operations appropriation measures: Development Assistance (DA), Child Survival and Health (CSH), the Global AIDS Initiative (GAI), the Economic Support Fund (ESF), Assistance for Eastern Europe and the Baltic States, Assistance for the Independent States of the former Soviet Union, and alternative development programs implemented through the Andean Counter-narcotics Initiative (ACI). Collectively, these programs total $8.1 billion, or roughly 40% of total FY2004 foreign aid appropriations.

As noted above, USAID organizes bilateral economic assistance around three functional "strategic pillars," allocating resources to each of 14 more specific program sectors within the three pillars. Changes in the amount of funds distributed to each of these sectors is one means of measuring the relative priority placed by the executive branch on any of these specific bilateral aid activities. Because Congress closely examines the executive's sector distribution of bilateral economic resources and in a number of cases modifies the President's proposed budget plan, sector funding trends also characterize congressional aid priorities and areas of special concern.[6]

Global Health

One of the most striking changes in the distribution of economic aid resources in recent years has been the sharp growth in funding for Global Health, especially in the area of HIV/AIDS programs. The budget for Global Health has nearly doubled since FY2001, while HIV/AIDS resources have increased almost five-fold.[7] In FY2004, the Bush Administration launched a five-year, $15 billion Global AIDS Initiative, with the goals of 7 million new infections, treating 2 million HIV-infected individuals, and caring for 10 million infected people and AIDS orphans.

Funding for two other health sectors are rising, but far more modestly than HIV/AIDS programs. Child Survival and Maternal Health projects aim to reduce infant mortality by, among other interventions, decreasing the incidence of acute respiratory infections, diarrheal disease, measles, and other illnesses that occur in the first 28 days of life and combating malnutrition, and to improve the quality of child delivery facilities and raise nutritional levels of mothers. Funding for these activities has grown by 27% in the past four years. Congress has placed special attention on other infectious disease activities — mainly those addressing malaria and tuberculosis — increasing spending by 43% since FY2001.

Table 1. Bilateral Economic Assistance Sector Allocation FY2001-FY2004 (millions of dollars)

Aid "Pillars" and Sectors	FY2001	FY2002	FY2003	FY2004
Econ. Growth, Agriculture and Trade:	$3,595	$3,717	$6,278	$4,421
Economic Growth	$1,556	$1,485	$3,227	$2,447
Agriculture	$301	$440	$480	$409
Environment	$591	$504	$500	$483
Basic Education for Children	$119	$186	$271	$325
Higher Education	$176	$168	$186	$162
Other*	$852	$934	$1,614	$595
Global Health:	$1,280	$1,544	$1,899	$2,534
Child Survival/Maternal Health	$350	$408	$399	$447
Vulnerable Children	$41	$38	$34	$36
HIV/AIDS**	$305	$454	$855	$1,419
Other Infectious Diseases	$141	$178	$173	$202
Family Planning/Reproductive Health	$443	$466	$438	$430
Democracy, Conflict, and Humanitarian	$1,010	$1,078	$1,162	$1,198
Democracy and Governance/Conflict	$857	$941	$1,000	$1,051
Human Rights	$34	$40	$50	$44
Humanitarian Aid	$119	$97	$112	$103
TOTAL	$5,885	$6,339	$9,339	$8,153

* This Other category is label as programs of "Special Concern" by USAID, consisting of economic aid to Israel and Turkey, and obligations pursuant to the South Pacific Tuna Treaty. The composition of these "Special Concerns" may change from year-to-year, but do not necessarily fit into any of the categories under the pillar of Economic Growth, Agriculture, and Trade.
** Includes funds for USAID programs, the State Department's Global AIDS Initiative office, and the U.S. contribution to the Global Fund to Fight HIV/AIDS, Tuberculosis, and Malaria. Does not include funds provided by the Centers for Disease Control, the National Institutes for Health, and other "non-foreign aid" agencies.
Source: USAID.

This rapid rise in Global Health generally, driven largely by HIV/AIDS funding increases, however, overshadows to some extent reductions for other sectors. Spending on Family Planning and Reproductive Health programs has been relatively flat during the past four years, with the FY2004 level below that of FY2001. Vulnerable Children programs, meaning those that focus on children affected by war, street children, and children with disabilities, have also received flat levels of funding, and FY2004 amounts are about 12% less than FY2001.

Economic Growth

Within the "pillar" with the largest level of funding —Economic Growth, Agriculture, and Trade — the patterns have also been mixed. Basic Education programs, which encourage countries to strengthen their educational institutions and policies and reduce barriers for girls to attend school, have received nearly a three-fold increase in funding since FY2001. Resources for higher education, on the other hand, have declined slightly over the same period.

USAID has placed revitalized emphasis in recent years on Agriculture activities, an area which had been the largest program sector two decades ago. Funding rose by 50% in FY2002/2003 before falling back to a level in FY2004 that is one-third higher than FY2001. Agriculture programs focus on science and technology advances that reduce poverty and hunger, trade-promotion opportunities for farmers, and sound environmental management practices for sustainable agriculture.

Programs for managing natural resources and protecting the global environment have been the largest area of funding cuts since FY2001. These activities focus on conserving biological diversity, improving the management of land, water, and forests, promoting environmentally-sound urban development, encouraging clean and efficient energy production and use, and reducing the threat of global climate change while strengthening sustainable economic growth. Funding levels are nearly 20% below amounts in FY2001.

Resource trends for Economic Growth activities are more difficult to assess. This sector funds a wide range of development activities, focusing on trade capacity building, improving the investment climate, and promoting job creation, with an overall goal of reducing poverty. Budget support and commodity import programs are also included in this sector. Funding for Economic Growth programs has been affected by terrorism-related supplementals, especially large aid packages for Afghan reconstruction. This makes it difficult to identify any specific trend. Much of the increase for FY2003 came from additional assistance for several "front-line" states in the war on terrorism immediately prior to the launch of military operations in Iraq. The reduced amount for FY2004 (although still large compared with FY2001/2002) includes significant supplemental spending in Afghanistan for road construction and other economic rehabilitation activities.[8]

Democracy

Overall funding for the Democracy, Conflict, and Humanitarian "pillar" has risen by 20% since FY2001, with most increases coming in the area of Democracy, Governance and Conflict Prevention. Program goals include strengthening the performance and accountability of government institutions, combating corruption, and addressing the causes and consequences of conflict. Human Rights is a relatively small sector supporting a range of activities such as strengthening women's legal clinics and combating trafficking in persons. Funding levels have grown somewhat in recent years. Humanitarian Assistance under this "pillar" has declined in funding by over 10% since FY2001. Most of these programs are centered in Colombia and former Soviet states, concentrating on addressing the needs of internally displaced persons and conflict-affected communities.[9]

Which Countries Receive U.S. Foreign Aid?

In FY2004, the United States is providing some form of foreign assistance to about 150 countries. Figures 3 and 4 illustrate the top 15 recipients of U.S. foreign assistance estimated for FY1994 and FY2004, respectively. Assistance, although provided to many nations, is concentrated heavily in certain countries, reflecting the priorities and interests of United States foreign policy at the time.

As shown in the figures below, there are both similarities and sharp differences between country aid recipients for the two periods. The most consistent thread connecting the top aid recipients over the past decade has been continuing U.S. support for peace in the Middle East, with large programs maintained for Israel and Egypt. The importance of Latin America counter-narcotics efforts is also evident in both periods, with Bolivia, Peru, and more recently, Colombia, among the top U.S. aid recipients. Assisting countries emerging from conflict, usually under more temporary circumstances, is another characterization of U.S. foreign aid. The leading recipients of Haiti, Bosnia, and South Africa in FY1994 have been replaced currently by Liberia and Sudan.

But there are also significant contrasts in the leading aid recipients of the past decade. The most prominent is that Iraq is by far the largest recipient of U.S. assistance in FY2004 at $18.44 billion. The impact of the terrorist attacks on September 11, 2001, and the subsequent use of foreign aid to support other nations threatened by terrorism or helping the U.S. combat the global threat is clearly seen in the country-aid allocations for FY2004. Afghanistan, Pakistan, Turkey, Jordan, and Indonesia are key partners in the war on terrorism.

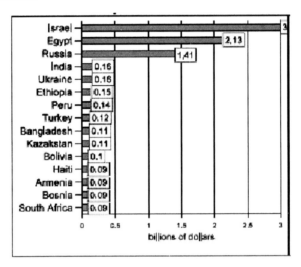

Figure 3. Top Foreign Aid Recipients, FY1994

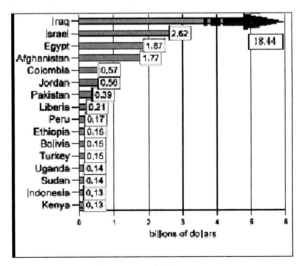

Figure 4. Top Foreign Aid Recipients, FY2004
Sources: USAID and the Department of State.

Another new feature of American assistance — the emphasis on HIV/AIDS programs — is evident in FY2004 aid figures with Ethiopia, Uganda, and Kenya among the top recipients, largely due to their selection as "focus" countries for the Administration's five-year, $15 billion Global AIDS Initiative. A further shift concerns the former Soviet states in which the United States invested large sums to assist in their transitions to democratic societies and market-oriented economies. In FY1994, four of these states were among the top 15 U.S. aid recipients. By FY2004, none are among the leading recipients and some are scheduled for "graduation" from U.S. assistance in the near term.

On a regional basis (Figures 5 and 6), the Middle East has for many years received the bulk of U.S. foreign assistance. With economic aid to the region's top two recipients, Israel and Egypt, declining since the late 1990s and overall increases in other areas, however, the share of bilateral U.S. assistance consumed by the Middle East fell from 58% in FY1994 to 38% a decade later.[10]

Since September 11, South Asia has emerged as region of growing concentrated levels of U.S. assistance, rising from a 4% share ten years ago to 17% in FY2004. Latin America, where a renewed effort to counter narcotics production and trafficking is bolstered with large aid programs, is a region where the proportion of total U.S. assistance has grown modestly. Similarly, the share represented by African nations has increased from 13% to 18%, largely due to the Global AIDS Initiative that concentrates resources on 15 (12 in Africa) "focus" countries where the disease has had the most serious consequences. With the graduation of several East European aid recipients in recent years and the phasing down of programs in Russia, Ukraine, and other former Soviet states, the Europe/Eurasia regional share has fallen somewhat. The proportion of assistance provided to East Asia grew in the past decade, but the region remains the smallest area of concentration, accounting for 3% of U.S. foreign aid in FY2004.

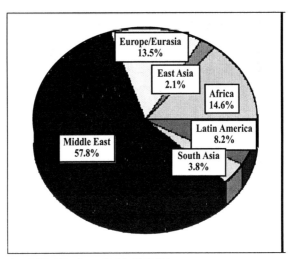

Figure 5. Regional Distribution of Aid, FY1994

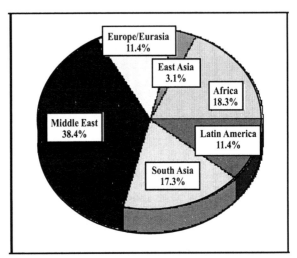

Figure 6. Regional Distribution of Aid, FY2004
Sources: USAID and the Department of State.

FOREIGN AID SPENDING

How Large is the U.S. Foreign Assistance Budget and What Have Been the Historical Funding Trends?

There are several methods commonly used for measuring the size of federal spending categories such as foreign assistance. Amounts can be expressed in terms of budget authority (funds appropriated by Congress), outlays (money actually spent), as a percent of the total federal budget, as a percent of discretionary budget authority (funds that Congress directly controls, excluding mandatory and entitlement programs), or as a percent of the gross domestic product (GDP) (an indication of the national wealth allocated to foreign aid).

By nearly all of these measures, some of which are illustrated in Figures 7 and 8, foreign aid resources fell steadily over several decades since the historical high levels of the late 1940s and early 1950s. This downward trend was sporadically interrupted, with spikes in the early 1960s and 1970s, 1979, and the mid-1980s, largely due to major foreign policy initiatives such as the Alliance for Progress for Latin America in 1961and the signing of the Camp David Middle East Peace Accords in 1979. The lowest point in U.S. foreign aid spending came in the mid-1990s whenresources fell to about $15 billion (in constant dollar terms) and represented roughly one-fourth of the total program size during the Marshall Plan period.

Following the September 11 terrorist attacks, foreign aid became a key instrument in fighting the global war on terrorism and contributing to the reconstruction of Afghanistan and Iraq.

Excluding economic and security aid for Iraq, total foreign assistance for FY2003-2004 has been larger than any two-year period since the mid-1980s. Including Iraq reconstruction costs — an amount that nearly equals all other foreign aid combined for FY2004 —the current two-year average represents the largest amount of foreign aid in thirty years, and is comparable to other foreign aid "surges" over the past half century, other than the Marshall Plan period. (Note: See Figure 9 at the end of this section for a more detailed "snapshot" of foreign aid funding trends and related foreign policy events.)

As a percent of gross national product, prior to the mid-1960s, in most years foreign aid represented over 1% and exceeded 2% during the Marshall Plan period. Following the end of the Vietnam War, foreign assistance as a percent of GDP ranged between 0.5% and 0.25% for the next 20 years. The program size dropped further to its lowest level ever in FY1997/1998 and

FY2001/2002 (0.16%). Foreign aid as a percent of GDP rose somewhat the past two years, averaging about 0.2% but remains near the all time low (Figure 8).

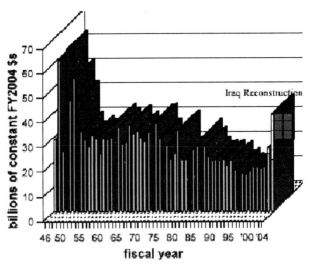

Source: USAID, OMB and CRS calculations.
Figure 7. U.S. Foreign Aid: FY1946 – FY2004

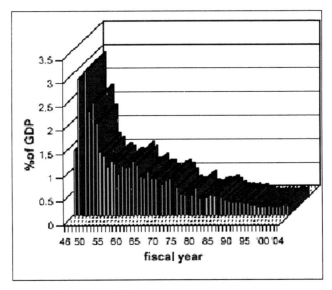

Figure 8. Foreign Aid as a % of GDP

Congress appropriates most foreign aid money through the annual Foreign Operations appropriations bill. Each year it represents the most direct congressional action on foreign assistance spending decisions, although small amounts of foreign aid are funded in other legislation.[11] Similar to the other measures of how much the United States spends on foreign assistance programs, Foreign Operations appropriations declined in the mid-1990s to slightly below $14 billion, the lowest level during the past decade in real terms (Table 2). Appropriated amounts rose beginning in FY1998 and averaged about $17.4 billion through the next four years. The combination of additional funding for the war on terrorism, Afghanistan reconstruction, and new foreign aid initiatives focused on HIV/AIDS and the Millennium Challenge Corporation, pushed average annual amounts, excluding Iraq reconstruction, above $20 billion in FY2003/2004. Including Iraq funding makes FY2004 the largest Foreign Operations appropriations, in real terms, in at least 30 years.[12]

Table 2. Foreign Operations Appropriations, FY1995 to FY2004 (discretionary budget authority in billions of current and constant dollars)

	FY94	FY95	FY96	FY97	FY98	FY99	FY00	FY01	FY02	FY03	FY04
Nominal $s	12.91	13.61	12.46	12.27	13.15	15.44	16.41	16.31	16.54	21.16	19.27
Constant FY04 $s	15.57	16.12	14.46	13.95	14.76	17.08	17.71	17.17	17.21	21.57	19.27

Notes: FY1999 excludes $17.861 billion for the IMF. FY2003 and FY2003 exclude funds for Iraq reconstruction. Including Iraq funds, FY2003 totals $23.67 billion in nominal terms and $24.15 billion in constant dollars. FY2004 totals $38.69 billion with Iraq funds.

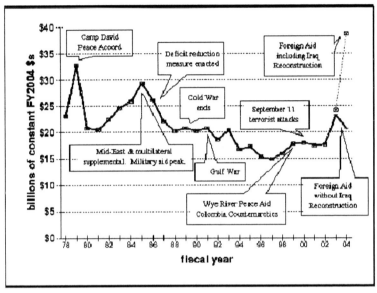

Figure 9. Foreign Aid Funding Trends, FY1978 - FY2004

How Does Foreign Aid Spending Compare with Other Federal Programs?

Foreign aid spending is a relatively small component of the U.S. federal budget. As part of the total amount spent in FY2004 on all discretionary programs (those controlled by Congress through appropriations), entitlements, and other mandatory activities, foreign aid outlays represent an estimated 0.9%, excluding expenditures for Iraq reconstruction. This figure is in line with typical foreign aid outlay amounts, which have generally equaled slightly less than 1% of total U.S. spending. With Iraq funding, FY2004 foreign aid outlays represent 1.2% of the entire budget. Figure 10 compares foreign aid outlays for FY2004 with those of other major U.S. government spending categories.

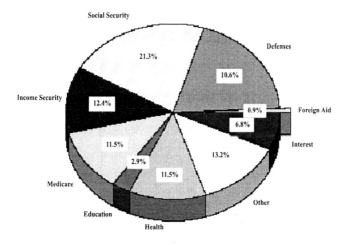

Source: OMB
Figure 10. U.S. Budget Outlays, FY2004

How Much of Foreign Aid Dollars Are Spent on U.S. Goods?

Most U.S. foreign aid is used for procurement of U.S. goods and services, although amounts of aid coming back to the United States differ by program. No exact figure is available due to difficulties in tracking procurement item by item, but some general estimates are possible for individual programs, though these may differ year to year.

In FY2004, roughly 87% or $3.7 billion of **military aid financing** will be used for procurement of U.S. military equipment and training. The remaining 13% are funds allocated to Israel for procurement within that country.

Food assistance commodities are purchased wholly in the United States, and most expenditures for shipping those commodities to recipient countries go entirely to U.S. freight companies. Under current legislation, three-fourths of all food aid must be shipped by U.S. carriers. On this basis, a rough estimate suggests that more than 90% — at least $1 billion in FY2004 — of food aid expenditures will be spent in the United States.

Because U.S. contributions to **multilateral institutions** are mixed with funds from other nations and the bulk of the program is financed with borrowed funds rather than direct government contributions, the U.S. share of procurement financed by MDBs may exceed the amount of the U.S. contribution. For example, the $1.88 billion in World Bank procurement from American sources for investment and adjustment loans in FY2003 (the most recent year for which data are available) was more than twice the $844.5 million U.S. contribution to the IBRD and IDA, the Bank's two largest facilities. The United States accounted for about 18% of all World Bank foreign procurement in FY2003, the largest of any country. Germany (7.8%), France (5.4%), Italy (5.1%), and China (4.9%) followed.[13]

Most **bilateral development assistance** and the **ESF, NIS and SEED components of economic political and security assistance** support programs in developing countries and the new European democracies, respectively. Although a small proportion of funding for these programs results in transfers of U.S. dollars, the services of experts and project management personnel and much of the required equipment is procured from the United States. According to USAID, 81% of total USAID procurement between October 2002 and September 2003 under these programs came from U.S. sources.[14]

Although some might argue that a greater proportion of U.S. foreign aid than is currently the case should be used for procurement of U.S. goods and services, a 100% level of reflows would be difficult if not impossible to achieve. Projects carried out in the developing world by their nature require a degree of spending within the recipient country — for local hire personnel, local building materials, and other operational expenses.

Many argue that the foreign aid program brings significant indirect financial benefits to the United States, in addition to the direct benefits derived from reflows of aid dollars. First, it is argued that provision of military equipment through the military assistance program and food commodities through P.L.480 helps to develop future, strictly commercial, markets for those products. Second, as countries develop economically, they are in a position to purchase more goods from abroad and the United States benefits as a trade partner.

How Does the United States Rank as a Donor of Foreign Aid?

For decades, the United States ranked first among the developed countries in net disbursements of economic aid, or "Official Development Assistance (ODA)" as defined by the international donor community. In 1989, for the first time, Japan supplanted the United States as the largest donor. The United States regained its leading position in 1990, only to lose it again in 1993 and fluctuated between a second and third position until 2001. In that year, it again became the largest contributor and remained in the position in 2002 with a contribution of $13.3 billion. Japan followed at $9.3 billion, significantly higher than France and Germany at $5.5 billion and $5.3 billion respectively. As a group, the 22 members of the OECD's Development Assistance Committee (DAC) representing the world's leading providers of economic aid, transferred $58.3 billion in 2002, up 7.2% in real terms from the year before.

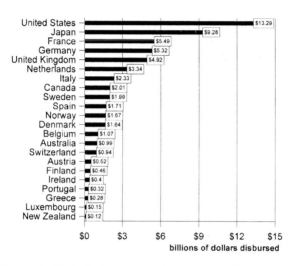

Figure 11. Economic Aid in Dollars from Major Donors, 2002

Even when it led in dollar amounts of aid flows to developing countries, the United States was often among the last when aid transfers by developed country donors were calculated by percent of gross national product. In 2002, as has been the case since 1993, the United States ranked last at 0.13% of gross national income (GNI). Denmark ranked first at 0.96% of GNI, while Japan dispensed 0.23%, France 0.38%, and Germany 0.27%. The average for all DAC members was 0.23%.

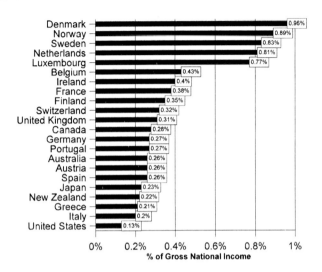

Source: OECD

Figure 12. Economic Aid as % of GNI from Major Donors, 2002

DELIVERY OF FOREIGN ASSISTANCE

How and in what form assistance reaches an aid recipient can vary widely, depending on the type of aid program, the objective of the assistance, and the agency responsible for providing the aid.

What Executive Branch Agencies Administer Foreign Aid Programs?

For over 40 years, the bulk of the U.S. bilateral economic aid program has been administered by the U.S. Agency for International Development (USAID) Created by an executive branch reorganization in 1961, USAID became an independent agency in 1999, although its Administrator reports to and serves under the "direct authority and foreign policy guidance" of the Secretary of State. USAID is responsible for most bilateral development assistance, including economic growth, global health, and democracy programs, Title II of P.L. 480 food assistance, and, in conjunction with the State Department, ESF, East European, and former Soviet aid programs. In FY2004, USAID manages a foreign aid budget of $12.65 billion, maintaining direct control over $5.7 billion of this amount. USAID's staff totals 8,132, of which only about 2,035 are U.S. citizens hired directly by the agency. The largest components of USAID staff are foreign nationals (3,570) working in overseas missions and representational offices who oversee the implementation of hundreds of projects undertaken by thousands of contractors, consultants, and non- governmental organizations (NGOs) Another 2,652 personal service contractors perform other work for the agency.[15]

In addition to these programs jointly managed with USAID, the State Department administers several other aid programs directly. Individual offices at the Department of State oversee activities dealing with narcotics control and international law enforcement, terrorism, weapons proliferation, non-U.N. peacekeeping operations, refugee relief, and voluntary support for a range of international organizations such as UNICEF. In order to manage the President's recent Global AIDS Initiative, the State Department has created a Special Coordinators Office that administers in FY2004 $488 million for international HIV/AIDS, tuberculosis, and malaria programs. These funds are expected to grow significantly in future years: the President has requested $1.45 billion for FY2005. The funds will be channeled through USAID, the Centers for Disease Control, the National Institutes for Health, and other implementing agencies. FY2004 appropriations for these State Department-administered aid programs totals about $2.75 billion.

Most military assistance is administered by the Department of Defense (DOD) in conjunction with the Office of Politico-Military Affairs in the State Department. The Defense Security Cooperation Agency is the primary DOD body responsible for foreign military financing and training programs. The Defense Department manages about $4.7 billion of total foreign aid spending in FY2004.

The Treasury Department also administers three foreign aid programs. U.S. contributions to and participation in the World Bank and other multilateral development institutions are managed by the Under Secretary for International Affairs. Presidentially appointed U.S. executive directors at each of the banks represent the United States point of view. Treasury also deals with foreign debt reduction issues and programs, including U.S. participation in the HIPC initiative. The Treasury Department further manages a technical assistance program, offering temporary financial advisors to countries implementing major economic reforms and combating terrorist finance activity. For FY2004, funding for activities falling under the Treasury Department's jurisdiction total about $1.5 billion.

A new foreign aid agency was created in February 2004 to administer the President's recently approved Millennium Challenge Account initiative. The Millennium Challenge Corporation (MCC) is charged with managing this results-oriented, competitive foreign aid delivery mechanism that will invest resources in countries that adopt pro-growth strategies for meeting political, social, and economic challenges. The MCC is a U.S. government corporation, headed by a Chief Executive Officer who reports to a Board of Directors chaired by the Secretary of State. The Corporation plans to maintain a relatively small staff of less than 200, while drawing on support from USAID. The MCC manages a budget of $994 million in FY2004, a total that is projected to grow to $5 billion by FY2006 under the President's plan.

Other government agencies which play a role in implementation of foreign aid programs are the Peace Corps, the Trade and Development Agency (TDA), and the Overseas Private Investment Corporation (OPIC). The Peace Corps, an autonomous agency with an FY2004 budget of $323 million, supports more than 7,800 volunteers in 73 countries. Peace Corps volunteers work in a wide range of educational, health, and community development projects. TDA finances trade missions and feasibility studies for private sector projects likely to generate U.S. exports. Its budget in FY2004 is $50 million. OPIC provides political risk insurance to U.S. companies investing in developing countries and the new democracies and finances projects through loans and guarantees. It also supports investment missions and provides other pre-investment information services. Its insurance activities have been self-sustaining, but credit reform rules require a relatively small appropriation to back up U.S. guarantees.

Two independent agencies, the Inter-American Foundation and the African Development Foundation, also administer U.S. foreign aid. Both organizations emphasize grassroots development by providing financial support to local private organizations in developing countries. For FY2004, Congress appropriated $16 million and $18 million to the Inter-American Foundation and the African Development Foundation, respectively.

Departing from the practice of using traditional U.S. aid agencies, such as USAID and the Departments of State and Treasury, Iraq reconstruction activities have been overseen by a new entity — the Coalition Provisional Authority (CPA). The CPA, which has received over $21 billion to undertake reconstruction projects in Iraq, is headed by a civilian administrator based in Baghdad but who reports to the President through the Secretary of Defense. The White House anticipates that the CPA will be dissolved on June 30, 2004, when governing authority is turned over to Iraqi interim government. It is further presumed that the State Department and USAID, which have been providing supportive work for the CPA, will take over responsibility for future Iraq reconstruction efforts.

What Are the Different Forms in Which Assistance is Provided?

Most U.S. assistance is now provided as a grant (gift) rather than a loan (see the next question for further discussion). But the forms a grant may take on its way to the recipient country are diverse.

Cash Transfers

Although it is the exception rather than the rule, some countries receive aid in the form of a cash grant to the government. Dollars provided in this way support a government's balance-of-payments situation, enabling it to purchase more U.S. goods, service its debt, or devote more domestic revenues to developmental or other purposes. Cash transfers have been made as a reward to countries that have supported the United States in its war on terrorism (Turkey and Jordan in FY2004), to provide political and strategic support (both Egypt and Israel annually since 1979), and in exchange for undertaking difficult political and economic reforms (multiple African countries since the 1980s, including Ghana, Mozambique, and Zambia in FY2004). Of FY2004 appropriations, about $855 million will be provided as cash transfers.

Commodity Import Programs (CIP)

The Commodity Import Program managed by USAID allows indigenous private sector business in a foreign country to gain access to U.S. dollars in order to import eligible American goods. In exchange for the dollars, local currency paid by these businesses goes to a host government account and is then programmed for development purposes by both the host country and the United States. The program, used widely in the past, is currently administered solely in Egypt and valued at $200 million in FY2004.

Equipment and Commodities

Assistance may be provided in the form of food commodities, weapons systems, or equipment such as generators or computers. Food aid may be provided directly to meet humanitarian needs or to encourage attendance at a maternal/child health care program. Weapons supplied under the military assistance program may include training in their use. Equipment and commodities provided under development assistance are usually integrated with other forms of aid to meet objectives in a particular social or economic sector. For instance, textbooks have been provided in both Afghanistan and Iraq as part of a broader effort to reform the educational sector and train teachers. Computers may be offered in conjunction with training and expertise to fledgling microcredit institutions.

Training

Transfer of know-how is a significant part of most assistance programs. The International Military and Educational Training Program (IMET) provides training to officers of the military forces of allied and friendly nations. Tens of thousands of citizens of aid recipient countries receive short-term technical training or longer term degree training annually under USAID's participant training program. More than one-third of Peace Corps volunteers are English, math, and science teachers. Other programs provide law enforcement personnel with anti-narcotics or anti-terrorism training.

Expertise

Many assistance programs provide expert advice to government and private sector organizations. The Treasury Department, USAID, and U.S.-funded multilateral banks all place specialists in host government ministries to make recommendations on policy reforms in a wide variety of sectors. USAID has often placed experts in private sector business and civic organizations to help strengthen them in their formative years or while indigenous staff are being trained. While most of these experts are U.S. nationals, in Russia, USAID has funded the development of locally-staffed political and economic think tanks to offer policy options to that government.

Small Grants

USAID, the Inter-American Foundation, and the African Development Foundation often provide aid in the form of grants that may then be used by U.S. or indigenous organizations to further their varied developmental purposes. For instance, grants are sometimes provided to microcredit organizations which in turn provide loans to microentrepreneurs. Through the USAID-funded Eurasia Foundation, grants are provided to help strengthen the role of former Soviet Union non-governmental organizations (NGOs) in democratization and private enterprise development.

How Much Aid is Provided as Loans and How Much as Grants? What Are Some Types of Loans? Have Loans Been Repaid? Why is Repayment of Some Loans Forgiven?

Under the Foreign Assistance Act of 1961, the President may determine the terms and conditions under which most forms of assistance are provided. In general, the financial condition of a country — its ability to meet repayment obligations —has been an important criterion for the decision to provide a loan or grant. Some programs — such as humanitarian and disaster relief programs — were designed from their beginnings to be entirely grant activities.

Loan/Grant Composition

During the past decade, nearly all foreign aid —military as well as economic — has been provided in grant form. Between 1962 and 1988, loans represented 32% of total military and economic assistance. This figure declined substantially beginning in the mid-1980s, until by FY2001, loans represented less than 1% of total aid appropriations. The de-emphasis in the amounts of foreign aid loan programs came largely in response to the debt problems of developing countries. Both Congress and the executive branch supported the view that foreign aid should not add to the already existing debt burden carried by these countries.

Types of Loans

Although a small proportion of total aid, there are several significant USAID-managed programs that provide direct loans or guarantee loans. Under the Israeli Loan Guarantee Program, the United States has guaranteed repayment of loans made by commercial sources to support the costs of immigrants settling in Israel from other countries. Other guarantee programs support low-income housing and community development programs of developing countries and microenterprise and small business credit programs. A Development Credit Authority in which risk is shared with a private sector bank can be used to support any development sector.

Loan Repayment

Between 1946 and 2001, the United States loaned about $108 billion under the foreign aid program. Of that amount, $68 billion had been repaid as of the end of FY2001, leaving nearly $29 billion outstanding.[16] Most recipients of U.S. loans remain current or only slightly in arrears on debt payments. For nearly three decades, U.S. foreign aid law (the so-called Brooke amendment) has prohibited new assistance to any country that falls more than one year past due in servicing its debt obligations to the United States. Afghanistan, Liberia, Somalia, Sudan, Syria, Zimbabwe, and Argentina are current examples of countries that are more than one year in arrears. The President may waive application of this prohibition if he determines it is in the national interest.

Debt Forgiveness

The United States has also forgiven debts owed by foreign governments and encouraged, with mixed success, other foreign aid donors and international financial institutions to do likewise. In total, the United States forgave or reduced about $17.1 billion owed by 46 countries between 1990 and 2002.[17]

In some cases, the decision to forgive foreign aid debts has been based largely on economic grounds as another means to support development efforts by heavily indebted, but reform-minded, countries. The United States has been one of the strongest supporters of the Heavily Indebted Poor Country (HIPC) Initiative. This initiative, which began in the late 1990s and continues in 2004, included for the first time participation of the World Bank, the IMF, and other international financial institutions in a comprehensive debt workout framework for the world's poorest and most debt-strapped nations.

But the largest and most hotly debated debt forgiveness actions have been implemented for much broader foreign policy reasons with a more strategic purpose. Poland, during its transition from a communist system and centrally-planned economy (1990 — $2.46 billion), Egypt, for making peace with Israel and helping maintain the Arab coalition during the Persian Gulf War (1990 — $7 billion), and Jordan, after signing a peace accord with Israel (1994 — $700 million), are examples.

What Are the Roles of Government and Private Sector in Development and Humanitarian Aid Delivery?

Most development and humanitarian assistance activities are not directly implemented by U.S. government personnel but by private sector entities. Generally speaking, government foreign service and civil servants determine the direction and priorities of the aid program, allocate funds while keeping within congressional requirements, ensure that appropriate projects are in place to meet aid objectives, select implementors, and monitor the implementation of those projects for effectiveness and financial accountability. At one time, USAID professionals played a larger role in implementing aid programs, but the affect of budget cuts on personnel and the emergence of private sector alternatives over the past thirty years has led to a shift in responsibilities.[18]

Private sector aid implementors, usually employed as contractors or grantees, may be individual "personal service contractors," consulting firms, non-profit non-government organizations (NGOs), universities, or charitable private voluntary organizations (PVOs). These carry out the vast array of aid projects in all sectors.

CONGRESS AND FOREIGN AID

What Congressional Committees Oversee Foreign Aid Programs?

Numerous congressional authorization committees and appropriations subcommittees maintain primary responsibility for U.S. foreign assistance. Several committees have responsibility for *authorizing* legislation establishing programs and policy and for conducting oversight of foreign aid programs. In the Senate, the Committee on Foreign Relations, and in the House, the Committee on International Relations, have primary jurisdiction over bilateral development assistance, ESF and other economic security assistance, military assistance, and international organizations. Food aid, primarily the responsibility of the Agriculture Committees in both bodies, is shared with the International Relations Committee in the House. U.S. contributions to multilateral development banks are within the jurisdiction of the Senate Foreign Relations Committee and the House Financial Services Committee.

Foreign aid *appropriations* are provided entirely through subcommittees of the Appropriations panels in both the House and Senate. Nearly all foreign aid funds fall under the jurisdiction of the Foreign Operations Subcommittees, with food assistance appropriated by the Agriculture Subcommittees.

What Are the Major Foreign Aid Legislative Vehicles?

The most significant *permanent* foreign aid *authorization* laws are the Foreign Assistance Act of 1961, covering most bilateral economic and security assistance programs (P.L. 87-195; 22 U.S.C. 2151), the Arms Export Control Act (1976), authorizing military sales and financing (P.L. 90-629; 22 U.S.C. 2751), the Agricultural Trade Development and Assistance Act of 1954 (P.L. 480), covering food aid (P.L. 83-480; 7 U.S.C. 1691), and the Bretton Woods Agreement Act (1945) authorizing U.S. participation in multilateral development banks (P.L. 79-171; 22 U.S.C. 286).[19] In the past, Congress usually scheduled every two years debates on omnibus foreign aid bills that amended these permanent authorization measures. Although foreign aid authorizing bills have passed the House or Senate, or both, on numerous occasions, Congress has not enacted into law a major foreign assistance authorization measure since 1985. Instead, foreign aid bills have frequently stalled at some point in the debate because of controversial issues, a tight legislative calendar, or executive-legislative foreign policy disputes.[20]

In lieu of approving a broad authorization bill, Congress has on occasion authorized major foreign assistance initiatives for specific regions, countries, or aid sectors in stand-alone legislation or within an appropriation bill. Among these are the SEED Act of 1989 (P.L. 101-179; 22 U.S.C. 5401), the FREEDOM Support Act of 1992 (P.L. 102-511; 22 U.S.C. 5801), and the United States Leadership Against HIV/AIDS, Tuberculosis, and Malaria Act of 2003 (P.L. 108-25; 22 U.S.C. 7601).

In the absence of regular enactment of foreign aid *authorization* bills, *appropriation* measures considered annually within the Foreign Operations spending bill has assumed greater significance for Congress in influencing U.S. foreign aid policy. Not only does the bill set spending levels each year for nearly every foreign assistance account, Foreign Operations appropriations also incorporate new policy initiatives that would otherwise be debated and enacted as part of authorizing legislation. The only foreign aid program not funded within the Foreign Operations measure is food aid, which Congress includes in the Agriculture appropriations bill.

DATA APPENDIX

Table 3. Aid Program Composition, 2004

Aid Program	$ - billions	% of total aid
Bilateral Development	$6.228	30.1%
Humanitarian	$2.550	12.3%
Multilateral Development	$1.702	8.2%
Economic Political/Security	$5.402	26.1%
Military	$4.791	23.2%
TOTAL	$20.673	100.0%

Source: House and Senate Appropriations Committees and CRS calculations.

Table 4. Program Composition, 1990-2004
($ - billions and % of total aid)

Fiscal Year	Development/ Humanitarian		Economic Political/Security		Military		Total
1990	$5.667	38.2%	$4.242	28.6%	$4.908	33.1%	$14.817
1991	$6.318	39.9%	$4.717	29.8%	$4.788	30.3%	$15.823
1992	$6.447	43.8%	$3.803	25.8%	$4.470	30.4%	$14.720
1993	$6.967	42.2%	$5.319	32.2%	$4.225	25.6%	$16.511
1994	$6.539	47.3%	$3.269	23.6%	$4.016	29.1%	$13.824
1995	$7.134	48.5%	$3.700	25.2%	$3.876	26.3%	$14.710
1996	$5.597	42.1%	$3.787	28.5%	$3.924	29.5%	$13.308
1997	$5.485	41.6%	$3.823	29.0%	$3.879	29.4%	$13.187
1998	$6.077	42.8%	$4.038	28.4%	$4.082	28.8%	$14.197
1999	$7.739	48.3%	$4.607	28.8%	$3.674	22.9%	$16.020
2000	$5.872	35.2%	$5.797	34.8%	$4.991	30.0%	$16.660
2001	$7.263	44.0%	$5.234	31.7%	$4.018	24.3%	$16.515
2002	$7.376	43.6%	$5.309	31.4%	$4.232	25.0%	$16.917
2003	$9.361	41.1%	$6.991	30.7%	$6.426	28.2%	$22.778
2004	$10.480	50.7%	$5.402	26.1%	$4.791	23.2%	$20.673

Sources: USAID, House and Senate Appropriations Committees, and CRS calculations.

Note: FY2003 and FY2004 exclude $2.475 billion and $18.439 billion, respectively for Iraq reconstruction.

Table 5. Foreign Aid Funding Trends

Fiscal Year	Billions of constant 2004 $	As % of GDP	As % of total discretionary budget authority
1946	$29.11	1.38%	— -
1947	$61.49	2.88%	— -
1948	$24.45	1.24%	— -
1949	$65.51	3.06%	— -
1950	$44.93	2.19%	— -
1951	$53.93	2.38%	— -
1952	$45.02	1.95%	— -
1953	$32.35	1.34%	— -
1954	$28.83	1.26%	— -
1955	$25.87	1.03%	— -
1956	$30.59	1.14%	— -
1957	$29.53	1.08%	— -
1958	$22.98	0.87%	— -

Table 5. Foreign Aid Funding Trends (cont.)

1959	$29.20	1.04%	— -
1960	$28.95	1.01%	— -
1961	$29.85	1.03%	— -
1962	$35.76	1.15%	— -
1963	$33.87	1.07%	— -
1964	$27.52	0.82%	— -
1965	$27.82	0.79%	
1966	$34.96	0.91%	— -
1967	$31.30	0.78%	— -
1968	$32.35	0.78%	— -
1969	$29.97	0.70%	— -
1970	$28.18	0.65%	— -
1971	$31.78	0.73%	— -
1972	$35.15	0.77%	— -
1973	$35.58	0.72%	— -
1974	$29.47	0.59%	— -
1975	$21.82	0.44%	— -
1976	$26.50	0.41%	—
1977	$21.26	0.39%	3.15%
1978	$23.13	0.41%	3.47%
1979	$32.75	0.55%	5.02%
1980	$20.78	0.36%	3.11%
1981	$20.47	0.34%	3.09%
1982	$22.40	0.38%	3.46%
1983	$24.67	0.41%	3.66%
1984	$25.90	0.40%	3.66%
1985	$29.30	0.44%	3.97%
1986	$26.15	0.38%	3.80%
1987	$22.04	0.31%	3.25%
1988	$20.25	0.28%	3.04%
1989	$20.74	0.27%	3.12%
1990	$20.23	0.26%	2.98%
1991	$20.73	0.27%	2.90%
1992	$18.62	0.24%	2.77%
1993	$20.31	0.25%	3.16%
1994	$16.67	0.20%	2.70%
1995	$17.31	0.20%	2.93%
1996	$15.35	0.17%	2.66%
1997	$14.92	0.16%	2.58%
1998	$15.92	0.16%	2.68%

Table 5. Foreign Aid Funding Trends (cont.)

1999	$17.71	0.18%	2.75%
2000	$17.97	0.17%	2.85%
2001	$17.42	0.16%	2.49%
2002	$17.58	0.16%	2.30%
2003	$23.22	0.21%	2.69%
2004	$20.67	0.18%	2.42%

Source: USAID, Office of Management and Budget, and CRS calculations.

ENDNOTES

[1] Other tools of U.S. foreign policy are the U.S. defense establishment, the diplomatic corps, public diplomacy, and trade policy. American defense capabilities, even if not employed, stand as a potential stick that can be wielded to obtain specific objectives. The State Department diplomatic corps are the eyes, ears, and often the negotiating voice of U.S. foreign policymakers. Public diplomacy programs, such as exchanges like the Fulbright program and Radio Free Europe, project an image of the United States that may influence foreign views positively. U.S. trade policy — through free trade agreements and Export-Import Bank credits, for example — are viewed as carrots by participating nations that affect the presence of U.S. business in those countries. Foreign aid is probably the most flexible tool — it can act as both carrot and stick, and is a means of influencing events, solving specific problems, and projecting U.S. values.

[2] U.S. Agency for International Development. *U.S. Foreign Aid: Meeting the Challenges of the Twenty-First Century.* January 2004.

[3] Because of the unanticipated nature of many disasters, humanitarian aid budget allocations often increase throughout the year as demands arise.

[4] Until FY1998, food provided commercially under long-term, low interest loan terms (Title I of P.L. 480) was also included in the foreign assistance account. Because of its increasing export focus, it is no longer considered foreign aid. Title I is administered by the Agriculture Department.

[5] This grouping excludes, however, counter-narcotics, anti-terrorism, the Millennium Challenge Corporation, other non-USAID/non-State Department programs, and agency administrative costs included in the totals for the two categories in Figure 1. In a sense, the category of aid discussed in this section represents what might be called "core" bilateral

economic assistance programs managed by the major U.S. foreign aid agencies.

[6] It is important to note that the amount of resources allocated to any single development sector is not necessarily a good measure of the priority assigned to that sector. Different types of development activities require varying amounts of funding to have impact and achieve the desired goals. Democracy and governance programs, for example, are generally low-cost interventions that include extensive training sessions for government officials, the media, and other elements of civil society. Economic growth programs, on the other hand, might include infrastructure development, government budget support, or commodity import financing, activities that require significantly higher resources. What may be a better indicator of changing sector priorities is to compare funding allocations over time to the same sector, trends that are illustrated in Table 1.

[7] The total U.S. government commitment to international HIV/AIDS programs is somewhat larger when the budgets for domestic, "non-foreign aid" agencies are included. For example, the amount for FY2004 is estimated to be $2.2 billion when the budgets of the Departments of Health and Human Services and Labor are included, rather than $1.4 billion drawn exclusively from State Department and USAID funding.

[8] Trends for the "Other" category in this pillar are also obscured by certain circumstances. These "Special Concerns," as labeled by USAID, fund cash transfer programs to Turkey and Israel, two strategic partners of the United States, and economic assistance to South Pacific island states under the terms of a fisheries treaty. Funding for these activities have been significantly influenced by supplemental appropriations related to the war on terrorism, especially in FY2003 when Turkey received a one-time $1 billion economic aid package. Absent special supplementals, this category is scheduled to decrease in future years as the United States phases out economic aid to Israel over a ten-year period.

[9] Much larger amounts of humanitarian assistance are provided through the separate accounts of emergency food aid under P.L. 480 Title II, USAID's Office of Foreign Disaster Assistance and Office of Transition Initiatives, and the State Department's refugee bureau. While these programs offer significant amounts of humanitarian aid — $2.4 billion in FY2004 — they generally respond to emergency, unanticipated situations and are not integrated into long-term development strategies managed by USAID.

[10] Including Iraq reconstruction funding for FY2004 would push the Middle East share to 73%.

[11] Most notably, food aid is not appropriated in the Foreign Operations measure, while the Export-Import Bank, an activity not considered "foreign aid," is funded in the Foreign Operations annual bill.

[12] Due to changes over time in appropriation "scoring" for various foreign aid programs, calculating precise levels of annual Foreign Operations appropriations that are equivalent to the methodology used currently is virtually impossible. This is especially true since Congress altered beginning in FY1992 the methodology for "scoring" credit programs. The 30 year estimate noted here compares the FY2004 level of $38.7 billion (including Iraq reconstruction) with total foreign aid amounts of about $35 billion (real terms) in the early 1970s. Since total foreign aid has not exceeded $31 billion (in constant FY2004 dollars) except for a period in the early 1960s and the years prior to FY1953, a reasonable estimate is that the current Foreign Operations appropriation, including Iraq funding, is larger than equivalent appropriations other than for these selected time frames. See Table 5 at the end of this report for complete data.

[13] World Bank Annual Report, 2003. Volume 2. Pages 132-140.

[14] The USAID figures, however, do not take into account that the U.S.-based contractor or grantee may spend some project funds in other countries. Because of this, actual procurement of U.S. goods and services may be much lower than indicated.

[15] USAID. *Congressional Presentation, Fiscal Year 2005*, p. 87.

[16] U.S. Agency for International Development. *U.S. Overseas Loans and Grants, July 1, 1945-September 30, 2001.*

[17] U.S. Department of the Treasury and the Office of Management and Budget. *U.S. Government Foreign Credit Exposure As of December 31, 2002*, part 1, p. 51.

[18] In 1962 there were about 8,600 U.S. direct hire personnel; currently there are about 2,000.

[19] Separate permanent authorizations exist for other specific foreign aid programs such as the Peace Corps, the Inter-American Foundation, and the African Development Foundation.

[20] A few foreign aid programs that are authorized in other legislation have received more regular legislative review. Authorizing legislation for voluntary contributions to international organizations and refugee programs, for example, are usually contained in omnibus Foreign Relations Authorization measures that also address State Department and U.S. Information Agency issues. Food aid and amendments to P.L.480 are usually considered in the omnibus "Farm bill" that Congress re-authorizes every five years.

In: Foreign Aid: Control, Corrupt, Contain?   ISBN 1-60021-067-8
Editor: A. A. Bealinger, pp. 41-62   © 2006 Nova Science Publishers, Inc.

Chapter 2

AGRICULTURAL EXPORT AND FOOD AID PROGRAMS[*]

Charles E. Hanrahan

ABSTRACT

The U.S. Department of Agriculture (USDA) forecasts that FY2004 agricultural exports will be a record $61.5 billion, exceeding the FY1996 record of $59.8 billion. Projected imports of $51.5 billion, also a record, will result in an export surplus of $10 billion, $500 million less than in 2003.

USDA operates four kinds of export and food aid programs that are authorized in the 2002 farm bill (P.L. 107-171), in the Farm Security and Rural Investment Act (FSRIA), and in permanent legislation. These programs include direct export subsidies, export promotion, export credit guarantees, and foreign food aid. Legislative authority for most of these programs now extends to the end of 2007. Export subsidies, but not other U.S. export and food aid programs, are subject to reduction commitments agreed to in multilateral trade negotiations.

Direct subsidies include the Export Enhancement Program (EEP) and the Dairy Export Incentive Program (DEIP). EEP spending has been negligible since 1996, but DEIP spending has been at the maximum allowed under international trade rules.

---

[*] Excerpted from CRS Report IB98006, dated August 23, 2004.

Market promotion programs include the Market Access Program (MAP) and the Foreign Market Development or "Cooperator" Program (FMDP). Considered to be non-trade distorting, these programs are exempt from multilateral reduction commitments. The FSRIA increases MAP to $200 million annually by FY2006 and sets FMDP spending at $34.5 million annually.

The FSRIA authorizes export credit guarantees by USDA's Commodity Credit Corporation (CCC) of $5.5 billion worth of farm exports annually plus an additional $1 billion for emerging markets through 2007. Actual levels guaranteed depend on economic conditions and the demand for financing by eligible countries.

The FSRIA also authorizes through FY2007 food aid programs including P.L. 480 Food for Peace, Food for Progress, the Emerson Trust (a reserve of commodities and cash), and a new international school feeding program. Section 416(b), permanently authorized in the Agricultural Act of 1949, also provides surplus commodities for donation overseas. Food emergencies in Africa and North Korea are putting pressure on the ability of food aid providers, including the United States, to meet estimated needs.

The House-passed FY2005 agriculture appropriations bill (H.R. 4766, H.Rept. 108-584) recommends an appropriation of $1.509 billion for USDA's international activities (discretionary funding), $12.2 million less than requested in the President's budget. With programs funded through borrowing from the Commodity Credit Corporation (other food aid and export programs), the estimated program value of all FY2005 international activities is $6.6 billion.

MOST RECENT DEVELOPMENTS

On July 13, 2004, the House passed the FY2005 agriculture appropriations bill (H.R. 4766, H.Rept. 108-584). The measure provides $1.509 billion for USDA's discretionary international programs, namely P.L. 480 food aid, the new McGovern-Dole International Food for Education and Child Nutrition Program (FEP), salaries and expenses of USDA's Foreign Agricultural Service, and administrative expenses for Commodity Credit Corporation export credit programs.

On February 2, 2004, the President transmitted to Congress his FY2005 budget. Included is a request for around $1.520 billion in discretionary funding for USDA international activities, mainly foreign food aid programs authorized in the Agricultural Trade Development Assistance Act (P.L. 83-480). The President's budget estimates that all USDA international activities in FY2005 (food aid plus mandatory food aid and export programs funded through borrowing from the Commodity Credit Corporation) will have a program value of around $6.6 billion.

On January 23, 2004, the President signed the FY2004 Consolidated Appropriations measure (P.L. 108-199) that includes annual funding for the U.S. Department of Agriculture and related agencies. The bill provides $1.512 billion for USDA's discretionary international activities.

BACKGROUND AND ANALYSIS

U.S. AGRICULTURAL EXPORTS

Agricultural exports are important both to farmers and to the U.S. economy. Production from more than a third of harvested acreage is exported, including an estimated 43.5% of wheat, 53.3% of rice, 43.1% of soybeans and products, 20.1% of corn, and 45.3% of cotton. About 25% of gross farm income comes from exports. Exports generate economic activity in the non-farm economy as well. According to USDA, each $1.00 received from agricultural exports stimulates another $1.47 in supporting activities to produce those exports. Agricultural exports generated an estimated 801,000 full-time civilian jobs, including 457,000 jobs in the non-farm sector in 2001. In contrast to the continuing overall trade deficit, U.S. agricultural trade has consistently registered a positive, though declining, balance.

Nearly every state exports agricultural commodities, thus sharing in export-generated employment, income, and rural development. In 2001, the states with the greatest shares in U.S. agricultural exports by value were California, Texas, Iowa, Kansas, Illinois, Nebraska, Minnesota, Washington, Indiana, and North Carolina . These 10 states accounted for 60% of total U.S. agricultural exports. In addition, Arkansas, Ohio, Florida, Missouri, Georgia, and South Dakota each shipped over $1 billion worth of commodities.

U.S. agricultural exports for 2004 are forecast by USDA to be a record $61.5 billion, exceeding the FY1966 record of $59.8 billion. Projected imports of $51.5 billion, also a record, will result in an export surplus of $10 billion, $500 million less than in FY2003.

The commodity composition of U.S. agricultural exports has changed over time with exports of high value agricultural products now exceeding those of bulk commodities. Since FY1991, bulk commodities (grains, oilseeds, and cotton) have accounted for less than total non-bulk exports (intermediate products such as wheat flour, feedstuffs, and vegetable oils or consumer-ready products such as fruits, nuts, meats, and processed foods). In FY2003, high value agricultural exports accounted for 63% of the value of total agricultural exports.

Many variables interact to determine the level of U.S. agricultural exports: income, population growth, and tastes and preferences in foreign markets; U.S. and foreign supply and prices; and exchange rates. U.S. agricultural export and food aid programs, domestic farm policies that affect price and supply, and trade agreements with other countries also influence the level of U.S. agricultural exports.

AGRICULTURAL EXPORT AND FOOD AID PROGRAMS

The trade title of the 2002 FSRIA (Title III of P.L. 107-171) authorizes and amends four kinds of export and food aid programs:

- Direct export subsidies;
- Export Promotion Programs;
- Export credit guarantees; and
- Foreign food aid.

USDA's Foreign Agricultural Service (FAS) administers the export and food aid programs, with the exception of P.L. 480 Titles II (humanitarian food aid) and III (food for development), which are administered by the U.S. Agency for International Development (USAID).

USDA International Program Activity, FY1996-FY2004
($ millions)

Program	1996	1997	1998	1999	2000	2001	2002	2003	2004 est.	2005 req.
EEP [a]	5	0	2	1	2	7	0	0	28	28
DEIP [b]	20	121	110	145	78	8	55	32	22	53
MAP [c]	90	90	90	90	90	90	100	110	125	125
FMDP [d]	—	—	—	28	28	28	34	34	34	34
GSM Programs [e]	3,230	2,876	4,037	3,045	3,082	3,227	3,388	3,223	4,275	4,528
P.L. 480 [f]	1,207	1,054	1,138	1,808	1,293	1,086	1,270	1,960	1,468	1,308
FEP [g]	—	—	—	—	—	—	—	100	50	75
Section 416(b) [h]	0	0	0	1,297	1,130	1,103	773	213	147	147

USDA International Program Activity, FY1996-FY2004 (cont.)

Program	1996	1997	1998	1999	2000	2001	2002	2003	2004 est.	2005 req.
FFP[i]	84	91	111	101	108	104	126	137	128	149
FAS[j]	167	191	209	178	183	201	198	195	199	212
Total	4,803	4,423	5,697	6,693	6,000	5,854	5,940	6,606	6,580	6,763

Sources: USDA, Annual Budget Summaries, various issues; the FY2003 appropriations act; and P.L. 108-199, the FY2004 appropriations bill.

a Export Enhancement Program.
b Dairy Export Incentive Program.
c Market Access Program.
d Foreign Market Development Program. FY1995-FY1998 FMDP spending included in FAS appropriation.
e GSM (General Sales Manager) Export Credit Guarantee Programs.
f The FY2003 estimate for P.L. 480 includes $1.326 billion for regular FY2003 appropriations; $248 million for Title II emergency assistance (after applying the across-the-board recision of 0.65%); and $369 million in the Emergency Wartime Supplemental Appropriations Act of 2003.
g The McGovern-Dole International Food for Education and Child Nutrition Program (FEP)was authorized in the 2002 farm bill; funds were first appropriated in P.L.108-199, the FY2004 appropriations bill
h Commodity value and ocean freight and transportation.
i Includes only CCC purchases of commodities for FFP. P.L. 480 Title I funds allocated to FFP are included in P.L. 480.
j Foreign Agricultural Service.

Export Subsidies

The FSRIA authorizes direct export subsidies of agricultural products through the Export Enhancement Program (EEP) and the Dairy Export Incentive Program (DEIP).

Export Enhancement Program (EEP)

EEP was established in 1985, first by the Secretary of Agriculture under authority granted in the Commodity Credit Corporation Charter Act, and then under the Food Security Act of 1985 (P.L. 99-198). The program was instituted after several years of declining U.S. agricultural exports and a growing grain stockpile. Several factors contributed to the fall in exports during the early 1980s: an overvalued dollar and high commodity loan rates under the 1981 farm bill made U.S. exports relatively expensive for foreign buyers; global recession reduced demand for U.S. agricultural products; and foreign subsidies, especially those of the European Union (EU), helped competing products make inroads into traditional U.S. markets. EEP's main stated rationale, at its inception, was to combat "unfair" trading practices of competitors in world agricultural markets.

The Office of the General Sales Manager in USDA's Foreign Agricultural Service (FAS) operates EEP. The Sales Manager announces target countries and amounts of commodities to be sold to those countries, and then invites U.S. exporters to "bid" for bonuses that effectively lower the sales price. An exporter negotiates a sale with a foreign importer, calculates the bonus necessary to meet the negotiated price, and submits the bonus and price to FAS. FAS awards bonuses based on the bids and amount of funding available. Initially awarded in the form of certificates for commodities owned by the CCC, bonuses since 1992 have been in the form of cash.

Most EEP bonuses have been used to assist sales of wheat. In FY1995, the last year with significant program activity, 72% of EEP sales were wheat, 8% flour, 6% poultry, and the remaining sales were eggs, feed grains, pork, barley malt, and rice. Although many exporters have received bonuses, since 1985 three exporting firms have received almost half of the total of all EEP bonuses which now exceed $7 billion. The former Soviet Union, Egypt, Algeria, and China were major beneficiaries of EEP subsidies.

The United States agreed to reduce its agricultural export subsidies under the 1994 Uruguay Round Agreement on Agriculture. The Agreement requires that outlays for export subsidies fall by 36% and the quantities subsidized by 21% over six years (1995-2001). Legislation to implement the Uruguay Round Agreement (P.L. 103-465) reauthorized EEP through the year 2001 and specified that EEP need not be limited to responses to unfair trade practices as in the 1985 Food Security Act, but also could be used to develop export markets. EEP was reauthorized in the 1996 FAIR Act and, most recently, in the FSRIA of 2002.

EEP has been a controversial program since it was initiated in 1985. Many oppose the program outright on grounds of economic efficiency. EEP, they argue, like all export subsidies, interferes with the operations of markets and distorts trade. Others, noting that the Uruguay Round Agreement on Agriculture restricts but does not prohibit agricultural export subsidies, point out that as long as competitors, such as the European Union, use export subsidies, the United States should also be prepared to use them. The effectiveness of EEP also has been an issue. Several studies have found that wheat exports would decline somewhat if EEP were eliminated, suggesting that EEP increases wheat exports. Other analysts, however, find that subsidized wheat exports under EEP displace exports of unsubsidized commodities such as corn.

Dairy Export Incentive Program (DEIP)

DEIP, most recently reauthorized in the 2002 farm bill, was established under the 1985 farm act to assist exports of U.S. dairy products. Its purpose was to counter the adverse effects of foreign subsidies, primarily those of the European Union. Early bonus payments were in the form of sales from CCC-owned dairy stocks; later they were generic commodity certificates from CCC inventories; now they are cash payments. As with EEP, USDA announces target countries and amounts of dairy products that may be sold to those countries under the program. Exporters negotiate tentative sales and "bid" for bonuses to subsidize the prices of the sales.

The Uruguay Round subsidy reduction commitments (see EEP above) apply also to DEIP. Uruguay Round implementing legislation authorized DEIP through the year 2001. The 1996 FAIR Act extended DEIP authority to FY2002, and FSRIA reauthorizes DEIP through 2007.

While many oppose subsidizing dairy products for reasons similar to those held by EEP opponents, the program has strong support in Congress. Dairy producers consider DEIP an integral part of U.S. dairy policy, an important adjunct to domestic support programs. That is perhaps why DEIP is reauthorized as part of Title I (commodity programs) of the FSRIA, not Title III (trade).

Market Promotion

USDA operates two market promotion programs, the Market Access Program (MAP), formerly the Market Promotion Program (MPP) which in its turn had succeeded the Targeted Export Assistance Program (TEA), and the Foreign Market Development Program (FMDP) also know as the "Cooperator" program.

Market Access Program (MAP)

TEA, authorized in 1985, was intended to compensate U.S. exporters for markets lost to unfair foreign competition. MPP/MAP is broader: its aim is to help develop foreign markets for U.S. exports.

MAP assists primarily value-added products. The types of activities that are undertaken through MAP are advertising and other consumer promotions, market research, technical assistance, and trade servicing. Nonprofit industry organizations and private firms that are not represented by an industry group submit proposals for marketing activities to the USDA. The nonprofit organizations may undertake the activities themselves or award funds to member companies that perform the activities. After the project is completed, FAS reimburses the industry organization or private company for part of the project cost. About 60% of MAP funds typically support generic promotion (i.e., non-brand name commodities or products), and about 40% support brand-name promotion (i.e., a specific company product).

The FSRIA authorizes MAP through 2007. The funding level for the program (previously capped at $90 million annually) gradually increases to $200 million by FY2006. The 2007 farm bill continues restrictions on the recipients of MAP assistance. No foreign for-profit company may receive MAP funds for the promotion of a foreign-made product. No firm that is not classified as a small business by the Small Business Administration may receive direct MAP assistance for branded promotions. Starting in FY1998, USDA's policy has been to allocate all MAP funds for promotion of branded products to cooperatives and small U.S. companies.

Foreign Market Development Program (Cooperator Program)

The FSRIA also reauthorizes this program through FY2007 with annual funding of $34.5 million. This program, which began in 1955, is like MAP in most major respects. The purpose of the program is to expand export opportunities over the long term by undertaking activities such as consumer promotions, technical assistance, trade servicing and market research. Like MAP, projects under the Cooperator Program are jointly funded by the government and industry groups, and the government reimburses the industry organization for its part of the cost after the project is finished. Like MAP, the Cooperator Program is exempt from Uruguay Round Agreement reduction commitments. Unlike MAP, which is more oriented toward consumer goods and brand-name products, the Cooperator Program is oriented more toward bulk commodities.

Some of the same issues raised with respect to MAP are also raised about the Cooperator Program and in some cases all the export programs. The basic issue is whether the federal government should have an active role in helping agricultural producers market their products overseas. Some argue that the principal beneficiaries are foreign consumers and that funds could be better spent, for example, to educate U.S. firms on how to export. Program supporters emphasize that foreign competitors, especially EU member countries, spend money on market promotion, and that U.S. marketing programs help keep U.S. products competitive in third-country markets.

Export Credit Guarantees

The FSRIA reauthorizes through FY2007 USDA-operated export credit guarantee programs, first established in the Agricultural Trade Act of 1978, to facilitate sales of U.S. agricultural exports. Under these programs, private U.S. financial institutions extend financing at interest rates which are at prevailing market levels to countries that want to purchase U.S. agricultural exports and are guaranteed that the loans will be repaid. In making available a guarantee for such loans, the U.S. government, or more specifically, the CCC, assumes the risk of default on payments by the foreign purchasers on loans for U.S. farm exports.

Export Credit Guarantee Programs (GSM-102 and GSM-103)

GSM-102 guarantees repayment of short-term financing (six months to three years) extended to eligible countries that purchase U.S. farm products. GSM-103 guarantees repayment of intermediate-term financing (up to 10 years) to eligible countries that purchase U.S. farm products. Eligible countries are those that USDA determines can service the debt backed by guarantees (the "creditworthiness" test). Use of guarantees for foreign aid, foreign policy, or debt rescheduling purposes is prohibited.

The 2002 farm bill authorizes export credit guarantees of $5.5 billion worth of agricultural exports annually through FY2007, while giving CCC flexibility to determine the allocation between short and intermediate term programs. The actual level of guarantees depends on market conditions and the demand for financing by eligible (i.e., creditworthy) countries. A provision in the statute allows guarantees to be used when the bank issuing the underlying letter of credit is located in a country other than the importing country. The new farm bill continues the provision that minimum amounts of credit guarantees would be made available for processed and high-value products through 2007. The farm bill permits credit guarantees for high-value products with at least 90% U.S. content by weight, allowing for some components of foreign origin. The legislation provides for an additional $1 billion through 2007 in export credit guarantees targeted to "emerging markets," countries that are in the process of becoming commercial markets for U.S. agricultural products.

The General Sales Manager in FAS administers GSM-102 and -103. U.S. financial institutions providing loans to countries for the purchase of U.S. agricultural commodities can obtain, for a fee, guarantees from the CCC. If a foreign borrower defaults on the loan, the U.S. financial institution files a claim with the CCC for reimbursement, and the CCC assumes the debt. If a country subsequently falls in arrears to the CCC, its debts may ultimately be subject to rescheduling.

The biggest recipients of export credit guarantees have been Mexico, South Korea, Iraq, Algeria, and the former Soviet Union (FSU). Iraq currently is in default of more than $3 billion of previously extended guarantees. Republics of the FSU, because they are less important as commercial markets for U.S. agricultural exports, are no longer major beneficiaries. In FY2002, the major recipients were Mexico ($595.3 million), Turkey ($395.4 million), South Korea ($379.7), China/Hong Kong ($189.5), and Algeria ($89.1 million). Guarantees have helped facilitate sales of a broad range of commodities, but have mainly benefitted exports of wheat, wheat flour, oilseeds, feed grains, and cotton.

The CCC can guarantee credits under GSM-102 for two other programs: "supplier credit guarantees" and "facilities financing guarantees." Under the former, the CCC will guarantee payment by foreign buyers of U.S. commodities and products which are sold by U.S. suppliers on a deferred payment basis. Under this variation of short-term credit guarantee, the foreign buyer alone will bear ultimate responsibility for repayment of the credit. The duration of the credit is short, generally up to 180 days, although the FSRIA permits guarantees of up to 360 days. These credits are expected to be particularly useful in facilitating sales of high-value products, the fastest growing components of U.S. agricultural exports.

The "facilities financing guarantee" is also carried out under the GSM-102 program. In this activity, the CCC will provide guarantees to facilitate the financing of goods and services exported from the United States to improve or establish agriculture-related facilities in emerging markets. Eligible projects must improve the handling, marketing, storage, or distribution of imported U.S. agricultural commodities and products.

The major issue concerning export credit programs is to what extent and how they might be treated in WTO agriculture negotiations. This issue is discussed below.

Foreign Food Aid

USDA provides food aid abroad through three channels: the P.L. 480 program, also known as Food for Peace; Section 416(b) of the Agricultural Act of 1949; and the Food for Progress Program. All these programs are authorized through FY2007 in the 2002 FSRIA, except Section 416(b) which is permanently authorized in the Agricultural Act of 1949. The FSRIA also authorizes the Bill Emerson Humanitarian Trust, which is primarily a commodity reserve, that can be used, under certain circumstances, to provide P.L. 480 food aid. The 2002 farm bill also establishes a new food aid program, the McGovern-Dole International School Feeding and Child Nutrition Program, which replaces a pilot activity, the Global Food for Education Initiative established in 2000 by the Clinton Administration.

P. L. 480 Food for Peace

P.L. 480, the Agricultural Trade Development and Assistance Act of 1954, has three food aid titles. Title I, Trade and Development Assistance, provides for long-term, low interest loans to developing countries for their purchase of U.S. agricultural commodities. Title II, Emergency and Private Assistance Programs, provides for the donation of U.S. agricultural commodities to meet emergency and non-emergency food needs. Title III, Food for Development, provides government-to-government grants to support long-term growth in the least developed countries. Title I of P.L. 480 is administered by USDA; Titles II and III are administered by the Agency for International Development (AID).

Private entities in addition to governments in developing countries are eligible to enter into Title I sales agreements. A five-year grace period may be granted before a recipient must begin repaying the principal on the credit extended under a Title I agreement. The Secretary could still allow up to 30 years for repayment, but could require repayment in fewer than 10 years if the recipient has the ability to repay in a shorter time. Priority for Title I agreements is accorded to developing countries with demonstrated potential to become commercial markets for U.S. agricultural commodities.

The P.L. 480 legislation allows private voluntary organizations (PVOs) and cooperatives to carry out Title II non-emergency programs in countries where USAID does not maintain a mission. FSRIA authorized funding to pay project or administrative and other costs of PVOs and coops at 5% to 10% of annual Title II funding. Previously, from $10 million to $28 million was available for these kinds of costs. Intergovernmental organizations, such as the World Food Program, also are eligible to apply for such funds. A minimum of 15% of non-emergency Title II commodities can be monetized (i.e., sold for local currencies or for dollars). Monetization enables PVOs and coops to defray the costs of distributing food or implementing development projects in countries where they operate. Currencies from Title II commodity sales (monetization) can be used in a country different from the one in which the commodities were sold, if the country is in the same geographic region. FSRIA stipulates that the annual minimum tonnage level provided as Title II commodity donations shall be 2.5 million metric tons, of which 1.875 mmt (75%) is to be channeled through such eligible organizations as private voluntary organizations, cooperatives, and the World Food Program.

Section 416(b)

This program, authorized in permanent law and administered by USDA, provides for the donation overseas of surplus agricultural commodities owned by the CCC. This component of food aid is the most variable because it is entirely dependent on the availability of surplus commodities in CCC inventories. Section 416(b) donations may not reduce the amounts of commodities that traditionally are donated to domestic feeding programs or agencies, prevent the fulfillment of any agreement entered into under a payment-in-kind program, or disrupt normal commercial sales.

Food for Progress (FFP)

FFP, first authorized by the Food for Progress Act of 1985 and also administered by USDA, provides commodities to support countries that have made commitments to expand free enterprise in their agricultural economies. Commodities may be provided under the authority of P.L. 480 or Section

416(b). The CCC may also purchase commodities for use in FFP programs if the commodities are currently not held in CCC stocks. Organizations eligible to carry out FFP programs include PVOs, cooperatives, and intergovernmental organizations such as the WFP. The 2002 FSRIA, as amended by P.L. 108-7, requires that a minimum of 400,000 metric tons of commodities be provided in the FFP program.

The Bill Emerson Humanitarian Trust

The FSRIA reauthorizes the Emerson Trust enacted in the 1998 Africa Seeds of Hope Act (P.L. 105-385). The Trust is primarily a reserve of up to 4 million metric tons of wheat, corn, sorghum and rice that can be used to help fulfill P.L. 480 food aid commitments to developing countries under two conditions: (1) to meet unanticipated emergency needs in developing countries, or (2) when U.S. domestic supplies are short. The Trust can also hold cash in reserve. The Trust, as presently constituted, replaced the Food Security Commodity Reserve established in the 1996 farm bill and its predecessor, the Food Security Wheat Reserve of 1980. The Trust, which the Administration recently tapped to meet urgent food aid needs in Africa and Iraq, has been used 10 times since its inauguration in 1980 — seven times to meet unanticipated needs and three times when domestic supplies were limited.

Mcgovern-Dole International Food for Education and Child Nutrition Program

The FSRIA authorizes this new food aid program, which can use commodities and financial and technical assistance to carry out preschool and school food for education programs and maternal, infant and child nutrition programs in foreign countries. Private voluntary organizations, cooperatives, and the World Food Program and foreign governments are all eligible organizations for carrying out these activities . FSRIA mandates CCC funding of $100 million for the program in FY2003 and authorizes appropriations of "such sums as necessary" from FY2004-2007. McGovern-Dole replaces the pilot Global Food for Education Initiative discussed below. By decision of the President, as mandated by the 2002 farm bill, USDA, rather than USAID, administers this program.

RECENT PROGRAM ACTIVITY

Export Subsidies

Although almost always under some pressure from interested commodity groups to use EEP more extensively, USDA has limited its scope and funding since 1995. The rationale for not using EEP is based on the argument that using it in the current international economic environment might depress wheat and other commodity prices now on the increase from lows reached in the late 1990s. Some analysts say that not using EEP also strengthens the U.S. hand in on-going WTO agriculture negotiations where a major U.S. aim is the elimination of agricultural export subsidies.

In FY1995, the last year of significant program activity, EEP bonuses were valued at $339 million. In FY1996, $5 million in EEP bonuses were awarded and none were awarded in FY1997. In FY1998, EEP bonuses amounted to just $2 million. Expenditures for EEP sales in FY1999 totaled $1 million. EEP bonuses of $2 million were awarded in FY2000. For FY2001, $7 million of EEP bonuses were awarded. No EEP bonuses were awarded in FYs 2002 or 2003.

Recent levels of DEIP reflect limits imposed by Uruguay Round Agreement commitments, an end to the "roll-over" authority in the Agricultural Agreement, which allowed countries to draw on unused subsidy authority from previous years, and world market conditions for skim milk powder. The program level for DEIP in FY2003 was $32 million and is estimated to be $22 million in FY2004.

Market Development

MAP, like EEP, is not funded by annual appropriations, but appropriations bills have on occasion capped the amounts that could be spent on the program. For example, the FY1999 agricultural appropriations legislation imposed no limits on MAP funding, but did prohibit MAP spending in support of promotion of exports of mink pelts or garments, a provision that was first adopted in the FY1996 agriculture appropriations bill. Since 1993, no MAP funds may be used to promote tobacco exports. Some Members of Congress targeted MAP for cuts in FY2000 to help offset increased expenditures on other programs, but such amendments were defeated. MAP was unsuccessfully targeted by budget cutters in FY2001 as well. USDA's allocation of $100 million for MAP funding in FY2002 is the full amount authorized in the 1996 farm bill plus $10 million authorized by the 2002 farm bill. A proposed amendment to eliminate completely MAP funding in FY2002 was defeated during floor consideration of H.R. 2330, the House-passed version of FY2002 agriculture appropriations.

Prior to FY2000, FMDP was funded as part of the appropriation of the Foreign Agricultural Service. The 1996 farm bill provided new statutory authority for the Program and authorized it through 2002. In FY2000, USDA moved funding for FMDP from discretionary to CCC funding, thus shifting its funding into the mandatory category. Funds allocated for FMDP in FY2001 were $28 million and USDA allocated the farm-bill authorized amount of $34 million for the program in FY2002, FY2003, and FY2004.

Export Credit Guarantees

For FY2003 export credit guarantees financed an estimated $3.2 billion of U.S. agricultural exports. FY2004 guarantees are estimated to be $4.3 billion. The amounts of credit guaranteed each year depend on the demand for guaranteed financing of U.S. agricultural commodities by eligible borrowing countries.

Food Aid

P.L. 480 food aid averaged around $1.1 billion from 1996 to 1998. In FY1999, however, more than $1.8 billion in P.L. 480 food aid was provided. Although only around $1.1 billion was appropriated for P.L. 480 in FY1999, the final total included approximately $700 million of Title I food aid for Russia, which was financed by a transfer of funds from the CCC. The FY2000 program level for P.L. 480 was $1.3 billion, while FY2001 P.L. 480 spending was $1.086 billion and the FY2002 program level was $1.270 billion, including Emerson Trust releases valued at $175 million. In FY2003, the food aid program level spiked again as Congress appropriated more than $1.8 billion for emergency humanitarian assistance under P.L. 480 Title II to meet emergency needs in Africa, Afghanistan, and Iraq. Commodity donations under Section 416(b) were $213 million (commodity value and ocean freight and overseas distribution costs) in FY2003, consisting of surplus nonfat dry milk. In contrast, Section 416(b) donations averaged about $1 billion a year from FY1999 to FY2002. Such large donations were made possible following CCC purchases of over 8 million metric tons of surplus wheat and wheat flour in FYs 1999 and 2000.

Around $300 million of Section 416(b) commodities and CCC funding were used to launch a global food for education initiative (GFEI) in July 2000. Under the GFEI, USDA donated agricultural commodities for use in school feeding and pre-school nutrition projects in developing countries. USDA-approved projects were implemented by the UN World Food Program (WFP), private voluntary organizations, and eligible foreign governments. The GFEI was superseded by the McGovern-Dole International School Feeding and Child Nutrition Program authorized in the 2002 farm bill.

Emerson Trust

The Secretary of Agriculture announced releases from the Trust of 275,000 tons of wheat on June 10, 2002 and 300,000 tons of wheat on August 28, 2002. The wheat from the reserve was exchanged for an equal value of corn, beans and vegetable oil for use in humanitarian relief in southern Africa, where an estimated 14.4 million people needed emergency food aid to compensate for severe food shortages and stave off famine through much of 2003. In FY2003, the Secretary announced releases of 200,000 metric tons for emergency food needs in Eritrea and Ethiopia and 600,000 metric tons for emergency needs in Iraq. Of the announced releases, only about half, 400,000 metric tons, were used. At present, according to USDA, 1.6 million metric tons and $107 million remain in the Trust. Partial replenishment of the Trust was addressed in the FY2003 Emergency Wartime Supplemental Appropriations Act (see below).

FY2004 APPROPRIATIONS FOR INTERNATIONAL ACTIVITIES

P.L. 108-199, the Consolidated Appropriations bill for FY2004, provides $1.512 billion for USDA's discretionary programs, namely P.L. 480 food aid, the new McGovern-Dole International Food for Education Program (FEP), salaries and expenses of USDA's Foreign Agricultural Service, and administrative expenses for CCC export programs. For the mandatory programs, which include both agricultural export and other food aid programs, the Administration estimates a program level of around $4.66 billion. Both the discretionary and mandatory international programs are authorized in the 2002 farm bill (P.L. 107-171). The appropriations bill places no additional funding limits on the mandatory agricultural trade and food aid programs.

The recommended appropriations for food aid is more than $600 million less than appropriated in FY2003. FY2003 appropriations included congressionally initiated responses to humanitarian food needs of $248 million for additional emergency food relief and $369 million for P.L. 480 Title II programs in the Emergency Supplemental Wartime Appropriations Act. The Senate report, accompanying the FY2004 appropriations measure, indicates that funding for P.L. 480 Title II should be used for its intended purposes, which it identifies as addressing underlying causes of hunger, and not for ad hoc emergency assistance. In the event of additional emergency needs, the report says, "the Committee reminds the Department of the availability of the Bill Emerson Trust."

The Consolidated Appropriations bill provides an appropriation for the first time for the McGovern-Dole International Food for Education Program and Child Nutrition Program (FEP). FEP will provide commodity donations and associated finance and technical assistance to carry out school and child feeding programs in foreign countries. The 2002 farm bill authorized $100 million of CCC funding for FEP in FY2003. Beginning in FY2004, however, the farm bill called for FEP to be funded by appropriations. The Senate Committee report, accompanying its version of the FY2004 agriculture appropriations, however, suggested that the Secretary investigate the use of Food for Progress resources for FEP to supplement appropriated funds.

The President's budget provides no estimate of the value or volume of commodities that could be released from the Emerson Trust in FY2004. The President's budget envisions $151 million of CCC funding for FFP; some funding for FFP also will come from appropriations for P.L. 480 Title I (concessional sales), for which the FY2004 bill appropriates $132 million. USDA estimates that about $119 million of surplus nonfat dry milk will be made available under Section 416(b) in FY2004.

The President's budget assumes a program level of $28 million in FY2004 for EEP. The 2002 farm bill, however, allows EEP spending of $478 million, which is the maximum allowed under the World Trade Organization/Uruguay Round agreement on subsidy reduction commitments. Thus, USDA retains some flexibility to increase the level of EEP subsidies in FY2004. For DEIP, the budget expects a program level of $57 million for FY2004, an increase above the $36 million estimated for FY2003.

The budget request assumes that the CCC will guarantee commercial financing of $4.2 billion of U.S. agricultural exports in FY2004. The anticipated level for each credit program is: GSM-102 ($3.4 billion); GSM-103 ($18 million); supplier credit guarantees ($750 million); and facility financing guarantees ($44 million).

Consistent with the farm bill reauthorization of MAP, the budget provides for MAP funding of $125 million in FY2004. The budget assumes the farm bill-authorized level of $34.5 million for FMDP in FY2004. The budget provides $2.5 million for a Quality Samples Program and $2 million for a new Technical Assistance for Specialty Crops Program to address phytosanitary and related technical trade barriers.

THE FY2005 BUDGET DEVELOPMENTS

The President's FY2005 budget request estimates that USDA's international activities, including both discretionary and mandatory programs, will have a program value of $6.6 billion for FY2005, up about $100 million from the FY2004 Administration estimate. Of that amount, approximately $1.5 billion would require budget authority in appropriations legislation, with the balance funded through the borrowing authority of the Commodity Credit Corporation.

For P.L. 480, the President requested budget authority of $1.294 billion for FY2005, $22 million less than the enacted amount in FY2004. Most of the FY2005 request, an estimated $1.185 billion, would be allocated to humanitarian commodity donations under P.L. 480 Title II, and is identical to the amount enacted in FY2004. The rest of the P.L. 480 request, $109 million, would be allocated to P.L. 480 Title I (direct commodity sales). The FY2004 appropriation for Title I was $131 million. The President's budget requests $75 million for FEP, $25 million greater than enacted in the previous fiscal year. The other major discretionary account is the Foreign Agricultural Service (FAS), for which the Administration requests an FY2005 appropriation of $143 million, up almost $12 million from the FY2003 appropriation.

The House passed its version of FY2005 agriculture appropriations (H.R. 4766, H.Rept. 108-584) on July 13, 2004. The measure provides $1.509 billion for USDA's discretionary international programs, namely P.L. 480 food aid, the new McGovern-Dole International Food for Education and Child Nutrition Program (FEP), salaries and expenses of USDA's Foreign Agricultural Service, and administrative expenses for Commodity Credit

Corporation export credit programs. For P.L. 480, the House committee recommends an appropriation of $1.291 billion for FY2005, $27 million less than enacted in FY2004 and $7 million less than requested by the President. Of the FY2005 recommended amount, the House committee allocated $1.180 billion to humanitarian commodity donations under P.L. 480 Title II. The Title II appropriation is $5 million less than the FY2004 enacted amount and $5 million less than requested by the President. For P.L. 480 Title I (direct commodity sales), the committee's recommended appropriation is $109.1 million, which is identical to the amount requested by the President, but $22 million less than enacted in FY2004. The recommended increase of $25 million in the appropriation for FEP (a total of $75 million recommended for FY2005) is largely offset by the reductions in P.L. 480 Titles I and II.

The other major discretionary account is the Foreign Agricultural Service (FAS), for which the House bill recommends an FY2005 appropriation of $137.7 million, down more than $6 million from FY2004's enacted amount and $5.3 million less than the President requested. FAS administers all of USDA's international activities with the exception of P.L. 480 Title II, administered by the U.S. Agency for International Development (USAID). The committee also recommends $4.5 million to cover administrative expenses of CCC export credit guarantee programs. The President's budget estimated that in FY2005, these administrative costs would support programs that finance $4.5 billion of U.S. agricultural exports.

Other food aid programs are mandatory (i.e., an annual appropriation is not required), including Food for Progress (FFP), the Bill Emerson Humanitarian Trust, and Section 416(b) commodity donations. The President's budget envisions $149 million of CCC funding for FFP. That program level (plus some funding from P.L. 480 Title I) is expected to provide the minimum 400,000 tons of commodities in FFP established in the 2002 farm bill. No commodities were released from the Emerson Trust in FY2004, but in FY2003, $212 million of commodities and related services were provided via the trust, which is primarily a commodity reserve used to meet unanticipated food aid needs or to meet food aid commitments if domestic supplies are unavailable. The President's budget makes no estimate of releases from the trust in FY2005, but notes that 500,000 tons are available for emergency food assistance. Around 1.6 million metric tons of wheat and $109 million in cash are currently in the trust. For Section 416(b) commodity donations, the President's budget projects a program level of $147 million ($15 million for ocean freight and overseas distribution costs and $132 million in commodity value). USDA indicates that only nonfat dry milk will be available for distribution under this program in FY2005.

A number of USDA's export-related programs are also mandatory and thus do not require an appropriation. Under the Export Enhancement Program (EEP) and the Dairy Export Incentive Program (DEIP), USDA makes cash bonus payments to exporters of U.S. agricultural commodities to enable them to be price-competitive when U.S. prices are above world market prices. EEP has been little used in recent years, and no EEP bonuses were provided in FY2004. Reflecting this program experience, the President's budget assumes a program level of $28 million in FY2005, compared with $478 million authorized by the 2002 farm bill. Consequently, USDA retains some flexibility to increase the level of EEP subsidies because of the mandatory authorization. For DEIP, the budget expects a program level of $53 million for FY2005, compared with a current estimate of $22 million for FY2004. For export market development, the budget proposes $125 million for the Market Access Program (MAP) and $34 million for the Foreign Market Development Program. Both these estimates are identical to amounts proposed in the FY2004 budget for USDA. The MAP request, however, is $15 million less than authorized in the 2002 farm bill. This proposed reduction could prove controversial, but the committee report does not address this issue. Most previous efforts at restricting MAP spending in Congress have met with little success.

TRADE NEGOTIATIONS AND
USDA INTERNATIONAL PROGRAMS

U.S. agricultural export and food aid programs could be affected by ongoing WTO agricultural trade negotiations. WTO member countries on July 30, 2004, reached agreement on a so-called framework for concluding the agriculture negotiations in the multilateral trade round knows as the Doha Development Agenda (DDA). The agriculture framework includes agreements that would affect the operation of U.S. export guarantee and food aid programs. (For details, see CRS Report RS21905, *The Agriculture Framework Agreement in the WTO Doha Round.*)

The agriculture framework stipulates that by "the end date" to be negotiated, WTO member countries will eliminate the following: export subsidies; export credits, credit guarantees, or insurance programs with repayment periods beyond 180 days; terms and conditions for export credits not in accordance with disciplines to be agreed, including, *inter alia*, interest payments, minimum interest rates, and minimum premium requirements; trade-distorting practices of exporting State Trading Enterprises (STEs); and provision of food aid not in conformity with disciplines to be agreed, including disciplines to prevent commercial displacement. However, WTO member countries will ensure that export credits, credit guarantees, or insurance programs "appropriately provide for differential treatment in favor of least-developed and net food-importing countries."

The elimination of EU export subsidies has been a long-standing objective of U.S. agricultural trade policy, as has requiring greater transparency in STEs such as the Canadian Wheat Board. Pressure from U.S. and developing country WTO members plus successive reforms of the EU's Common Agricultural Policy (CAP), which has reduced its reliance on export subsidies, led the EU to offer to eliminate them by a date certain. In exchange, however, the EU countered that all forms of export subsidies, including U.S. export credit guarantees and food aid, should be eliminated. This trade-off between export subsidies and export credit and food aid programs is reflected in the framework agreement. USDA's export credit guarantee programs, which have provided guarantees for about $4 billion of agricultural exports annually in recent years, would be substantially altered by the agreement. As presently constituted, these programs can provide credit guarantees from 180 days to 10 years (see program details above).

U.S. food aid for humanitarian relief and development projects (e.g., P.L. 480 Title II donations) that meet the criterion of not displacing commercial sales appear to be unaffected by the framework agreement. Earlier versions of the framework implied that commodity food aid would be eliminated in favor of cash grants. However, the framework does indicate that "(t)he question of providing food aid exclusively in fully grant form" will be addressed in the negotiations. The role of international organizations vis-a-vis WTO member countries' food aid programs will also be addressed in the negotiations.

Many in the U.S. agricultural community have expressed concerns that what they regard as effective tools for expanding agricultural exports (the CCC export credit guarantee programs) and providing food aid not be adversely affected by trade negotiations. The Trade Act of 2002, which contains negotiating objectives for U.S. participation in the current round of multilateral trade negotiations in the WTO (P.L. 107-210), makes preservation of export credit programs (and food aid) a principal negotiating objective. This objective calls for eliminating agricultural export subsidies, but maintaining bona fide food aid programs and preserving U.S. market development and export credit programs. Any changes in these farm bill export and food aid programs made necessary by a DDA trade agreement would be debated if and when Congress took up legislation to implement the agreement. Conclusion of the DDA negotiations could also occur as Congress begins deliberation on a farm bill to replace the 2002 FSRIA. DDA implications for export credit and food aid programs could thus be taken up in farm bill debate.

In: Foreign Aid: Control, Corrupt, Contain?   ISBN 1-60021-067-8
Editor: A. A. Bealinger, pp. 63-100   © 2006 Nova Science Publishers, Inc.

Chapter 3

MILLENNIUM CHALLENGE ACCOUNT: IMPLEMENTATION OF A NEW U.S. FOREIGN AID INITIATIVE[*]

Larry Nowels

ABSTRACT

In a speech on March 14, 2002, President Bush outlined a proposal for a major new U.S. foreign aid initiative. The program, referred to as the Millennium Challenge Account (MCA), is managed by a new Millennium Challenge Corporation (MCC) and provides assistance, through a competitive selection process, to developing nations that are pursing political and economic reforms in three areas: ruling justly, investing in people, and fostering economic freedom. If fully implemented, the initiative would represent one of the largest increases in foreign aid spending in half a century, outpaced only by the Marshall Plan following World War II and the Latin America-focused Alliance for Progress in the early 1960s.

The MCC differs in several respects from past and current U.S. aid practices:

- the size of the $5 billion commitment;
- the competitive process that rewards countries for past and current actions measured by 16 objective performance indicators;

---

[*] Excerpted from CRS Report RL32427, dated July 1, 2005.

- the pledge to segregate the funds from U.S. strategic foreign policy objectives that often strongly influence where U.S. aid is spent; and
- the requirement to solicit program proposals developed solely by qualifying countries with broad-based civil society involvement.

The Administration sought $1.3 billion for the MCA's first year (FY2004), $2.5 billion for FY2005, amounts reduced by Congress to a combined $2.48 billion, about one-third less requested. The President seeks $3 billion for FY2006, double the FY2005 level but less than the original $5 billion commitment for the third year.

Following the establishment of the MCC in P.L. 108-199 (January 23, 2004), the new Corporation formed, issued required reports, consulted with Congress and the public, and selected on May 6 and November 8, 2004, eligible countries for FY2004 and FY2005, respectively. Other MCA implementation matters have been unfolding since, including the relationship of MCA and USAID, how to support "threshold" countries, and funding programs, or "compacts," for those qualified under the FY2004 selection process. The Corporation signed the first Compact with Madagascar on April 18, 2005, and a second with Honduras on June 13.

A growing question raised by some Members of Congress concerns the level of funding to support MCC programs. Some, noting that proposals received by the Corporation in 2004 totaled more than $4.2 billion, fear that insufficient funds might force the MCC to reduce the number of recipients or the size of the grants. Others, however, believe that the slower-than-anticipated pace of Compact agreements means that the Corporation has or will have enough resources, and support reductions to the $3 billion FY2006 request. The Foreign Operations Appropriations, as passed the House (H.R. 3057), recommends $1.75 billion for MCC programs next year, while the Senate Appropriations Committee proposes $1.8 billion (also H.R. 3057).

MOST RECENT DEVELOPMENTS

On June 30, 2005, the Senate Appropriations Committee recommended (H.R. 3057; S.Rept. 109-96) $1.8 billion for the Millennium Challenge Account in FY2006, $312 million higher than in FY2005 but $1.2 billion less than the President requested.

On the previous day (June 28), the House passed the FY2006 Foreign Operations Appropriations measure (H.R. 3057) providing $1.75 billion to fund the MCA, slightly less than the Senate recommendation.

On June 15, Paul Applegarth, CEO of the Millennium Challenge Corporation, announced his resignation. No reason has been given for his departure, nor has the precise date on which he will leave been announced.

On June 13, President Bush met with the leaders of five African nations who raised concerns about the delays in implementing MCA country programs. President Bush pledged that the United States would work "harder and faster to certify countries."

On June 13, Honduras became the second country to sign an MCA Compact with the United States, a five year, $215 million program focused on rural agriculture development and road construction. Earlier, Madagascar signed the first MCA Compact on April 18, a four-year, $110 million program supporting land titling, financial sector support, and rural development projects. Also on June 13, the MCC Board of directors approved two other Compacts for Cape Verde and Nicaragua.

OVERVIEW

In a speech on March 14, 2002, President Bush outlined a proposal for the United States to increase foreign economic assistance beginning in FY2004 so that by FY2006 American aid would be $5 billion higher than three years earlier. The funds, referred to as the Millennium Challenge Account (MCA), is managed by a new Millennium Challenge Corporation (MCC) providing assistance, through a competitive selection process, to developing nations that are pursing political and economic reforms in three areas:

- Ruling justly — promoting good governance, fighting corruption, respecting human rights, and adhering to the rule of law.
- Investing in people — providing adequate health care, education, and other opportunities promoting an educated and healthy population.
- Fostering enterprise and entrepreneurship — promoting open markets and sustainable budgets.

If fully implemented, the initiative would represent one of the largest increases in foreign aid spending in half a century, outpaced only by the

Marshall Plan following World War II and the Latin America-focused Alliance for Progress in the early 1960s. It would also represent a fundamental change in the way the United States invests and delivers economic assistance.

While the program was established and initially funded during the 108th Congress, the 109th Congress is debating a major appropriation increase — to $3 billion — proposed for the MCA. Committees of jurisdiction have held several oversight hearings, and could consider changes to the authorizing legislation concerning such matters as selection criteria and methodology, operation and funding of the "threshold" programs for those countries that just missed qualifying for MCA grants, and program monitoring and oversight. Authorization for MCC operations in FY2006 are included in S. 600, as reported by the Senate Foreign Relations Committee. For funding matters, the House recommends a cut to the President's $3 billion request to $1.75 billion (H.R. 3057), while the Senate Appropriations Committee proposes $1.8 billion (also H.R. 3057).

MCC BACKGROUND[1]

The concept is based on the premise that economic development succeeds best where it is linked to free market economic and democratic principles and policies, and where governments are committed to implementing reform measures in order to achieve such goals. The MCC differs in several fundamental respects from past and current U.S. aid practices:

- the size of the $5 billion commitment;
- the competitive process that will reward countries for past actions measured by 16 objective performance indicators;
- the pledge to segregate the funds from U.S. strategic foreign policy objectives that often strongly influence where U.S. aid is spent; and
- the requirement to solicit program proposals developed solely by qualifying countries with broad-based civil society involvement.

The new initiative, which Congress authorized in January 2004 (Division D of P.L. 108-199),[2] is scheduled to phase in over a three-year period, beginning in FY2004. During the first year, MCC participation was limited to the 74 poorest nations with per capita incomes below $1,415 and that are eligible to borrow from the World Bank's International Development

Association. The list expanded in FY2005 to include all countries with a per capita income below $1,465 (adding another 13 nations). Beginning in FY2006 and beyond, all lower-middle income countries with per capita incomes below roughly $3,035 may compete for MCC resources.

Country selection is based largely, but not exclusively, on the nation's record measured by 16 performance indicators related to the three categories, or "baskets," of good governance, economic freedom, and investing in people. Countries that score above the median on half of the indicators in each of the three areas qualify. Emphasizing the importance of fighting corruption, the indicator for corruption is a "pass/fail" test: should a country fall below the median on the corruption indicator, it will be disqualified from consideration unless other, more recent trends suggest otherwise. (See Table 1 below for a complete list of the 16 performance indicators.) Administration officials, since announcing the MCC initiative in 2002, said that the selection process would be guided by, but not necessarily bound to the outcomes of the performance indicators. Missing or old data, general trends, and recent steps taken by governments might also be taken into account when annual decisions are made.

Eligibility to receive MCA assistance, however, does not necessarily result in an aid grant. Once selected, countries are required to submit program proposals —referred to as MCA Compacts — that have been developed through a broad-based, national discussion that includes input from civil society. The focus of program submissions may vary among countries in size, purpose, and degree of specificity, and are evaluated by the Corporation for, among other things, how well the Compact supports a nation's economic growth and poverty reduction goals. Only those Compacts that meet the MCC criteria will be funded. It is expected that successful Compacts will support programs lasting three to five years, providing a level of resources roughly equivalent to the largest providers of assistance in the country. This will most likely result in a significant increase of U.S. economic assistance to MCA participant countries.

To manage the new initiative, the Administration proposed and Congress authorized the creation of a Millennium Challenge Corporation (MCC), an independent government entity separate from the Departments of State and the Treasury and from the U.S. Agency for International Development (USAID). The MCC plans for an eventual staff of about 200, drawn from various government agencies, non-governmental organizations, and the private sector, and led by a CEO confirmed by the Senate. A Board of Directors, chaired by the Secretary of State and composed of the Secretary of the Treasury, the USAID Administrator, the U.S. Trade Representative, and the Corporation's CEO, oversees operations of the MCC and makes the country selections. Four additional Board members, two of which have yet to be confirmed by the Senate, are individuals from the private sector drawn from lists of proposed nominees submitted by Congressional leaders.[3]

The decision to house the MCA in a new organization was one of the most debated issues during early congressional deliberations of the President's foreign aid initiative. The Administration argued that because the MCA represents a new concept in aid delivery, it should have a "fresh" organizational structure, unencumbered by bureaucratic authorities and regulations that would interfere in effective management. Critics, however, contended that if the MCA is placed outside the formal U.S. government foreign aid structure, it would lead to further fragmentation of policy development and consistency. Some believed that USAID, the principal U.S. aid agency, should manage the MCA, while others said that the MCA should reside in the State Department where more U.S. foreign policy entities have been integrated in recent years. At least, some argued, the USAID Administrator should be a member of the MCC Board, which had not been proposed in the initial Administration request.

For FY2004, the Administration sought $1.3 billion for the MCA's first year, a level reduced by Congress to $994 million. The FY2005 budget proposed $2.5 billion while Congress approved $1.488 billion. The combined FY2004/2005 funding level of $2.48 billion is about one-third less than requested. The President initially planned a $5 billion MCA program by FY2006, but is proposing $3 billion for next year. Administration officials say that given congressional reductions the past two years and competing demands elsewhere, a $3 billion request is more realistic for FY2006.

MCC IMPLEMENTATION STEPS AND ISSUES

The passage of legislation on January 23, 2004 authorizing and funding the MCC for FY2004 (Division D of P.L. 108-199) launched a period of 90 days during which the new Corporation formed, issued required reports, consulted with Congress and the public, and selected first year participant countries. Within 10 days of enactment, the Board of Directors held its initial meeting to establish the program, and over the following weeks the Corporation identified "candidate" countries for FY2004, published the criteria and methodology to be used for country selection, solicited public comments, issued guidelines for Compact proposals, and, on May 6, 2004, selected 16 countries to participate in the MCA's first year of operations.

This was followed on November 10 with the selection of FY2005 eligible MCA countries, an action that added one new participant to the FY2004 list. An additional 13 countries have also been named as threshold nations — those that just missed qualifying as eligible countries.

Implementation matters that continue to unfold in 2005 include the relationship of MCC programs with those operated by USAID, how the Corporation and USAID will support threshold countries to better prepare for future performance reviews, the awarding of MCA grants — in the form of Compacts — to MCA eligible countries, and the funding request for FY2006.

Establishing the Millennium Challenge Corporation

On February 2, 2004, the Board of Directors met, agreed to Corporation bylaws, and approved then-Under Secretary of State Larson as the interim CEO. Subsequently, the President nominated Paul Applegarth to be the permanent MCC CEO, an individual confirmed by the Senate on May 5. CEO Applegarth has held various international and development positions over the past 30 years, primarily in the private sector. His most recent position prior to the MCC was the Managing Director of Emerging Markets Partnership, serving as the COO of Emerging Africa Infrastructure Fund in 2002.

Naming FY2004 Candidate Countries

Also on February 2, the MCC Board issued a list of 63 "candidate" countries that would be reviewed for possible selection as MCA participants in FY2004. These countries, according to authorizing legislation, must be eligible for assistance from the World Bank's International Development Association, have a per capita income of $1,415 or less, and not be otherwise ineligible to receive U.S. assistance. The latter condition eliminated twelve countries — Burma, Burundi, Cambodia, Central African Republic, Cote d'Ivoire, Guinea-Bissau, Liberia, Serbia, Somalia, Sudan, Uzbekistan, and Zimbabwe — that were statutorily barred from receiving American aid.[4]

Publishing the Selection Criteria and Methodology

Pursuant to reporting requirements set in the MCC legislation, the Corporation on March 5, 2004 sent to Congress an overview of the criteria and methodology that would be used to determine the eligibility of the 63 candidate countries in FY2004. The report suggested that there would be relatively few and only minor changes to the criteria and methodology that had been outlined 15 months earlier. The same 16 performance indicators, as listed in Table 1 below, would be utilized. In a few cases, data sources shifted from international institutions to national governments. This was especially true in cases where existing data for an indicator were old or incomplete.

Although the Corporation did not alter any of the original 16 performance indicators, it attempted to address additional criteria added by Congress in P.L. 108-199 through the use of supplemental data and qualitative information. While the legislative authorities broadly match criteria proposed by the Administration, lawmakers included four additional matters on which to evaluate a country's performance. These relate to the degree to which a country:

- recognizes the rights of people with disabilities;
- supports a sustainable management of natural resources;
- respects worker rights; and
- makes social investments, especially in women and girls.

For an evaluation of the rights of people with disabilities, the MCC reported that it would draw on information in the State Department's annual Human Rights Report, which includes a discussion of discrimination based on disability. Regarding natural resource management, the Corporation would also use the Human Rights Report as supplemental information on such issues as access to sanitation, deforestation, conservation of land and marine resources, land tenure institutions, and protection of threatened and endangered species. The State Department's Human Rights Report would also be used for additional information regarding worker rights, while statistics on girl's primary enrollment rates would supplement the four social investment performance indicators.

The MCC also noted that it would use the most recent release (then October 2003) of Transparency International's Corruption Perception Index to update and supplement the World Bank's survey data on which corruption performance indicator is based. This was necessary because the World Bank information was last published in March 2003. Since the corruption indicator is a "pass/fail" measure, the quality and timeliness of the data are especially important.

Given the range and diversity of suggestions offered throughout the public and congressional debate of the MCC, many observers were surprised that the Corporation did not propose more substantive changes to the criteria and methodology. Some questioned how seriously the Administration considered alternative approaches and whether the Corporation would be open to future revisions.[5] During the public comment period and at congressional oversight hearings, some suggested that existing data sources needed to be refined or new surveys created in order to specifically measure a country's commitment on the four criteria added by Congress.

After further study of the criteria and methodology, the Corporation announced on August 26, 2004, a revised set of performance indicators that were used for the FY2005 selection process. The MCC lowered the inflation rate threshold from 20% to 15%, making it somewhat more difficult to pass this test (only 6 of the 63 candidate countries failed this test for FY2004). An indicator measuring girls' primary education completion rates replaced a broader measure used in FY2004 that did not disaggregate primary education graduation by gender. As noted above, including the means to measure country performance on key women and girls issues was one of the requirements added by Congress during deliberation on MCC authorizing legislation.

The Corporation further indicated that it will explore additional criteria and methodology changes for FY2006. Under consideration are options to:

- lower the inflation level to 10%.
- identify a measurement related to natural resource management; the MCC has created a working group to study possibilities.
- review other possible indicators that would better measure trade barriers that are linked with economic growth.
- develop a more comprehensive indicator than the current Days to Start a Business to gauge a government's commitment to entrepreneurship and private-sector ownership.
- consider additional gender-relation indicators.

Future criteria and methodology is also likely to be affected by an amendment to MCC authorizing legislation approved by Congress in P.L. 108-477. Lawmakers added a more specific definition of the performance criteria related to "investing in people." In the future, this category will

extend to government policies promoting health and education, as the current
performance indicators attempt to measure, plus other factors contributing to
the well-being and productivity of its citizens, including access to affordable
housing.

Country Selection — FY2004

On May 6, the MCC Board of Directors determined that 16 countries
would be eligible for FY2004 MCA funding and invited each to submit
program proposals:

Armenia	Madagascar
Benin	Mali
Bolivia	Mongolia
Cape Verde	Mozambique
Georgia	Nicaragua
Ghana	Senegal
Honduras	Sri Lanka
Lesotho	Vanuatu

As expected, the selection process raised a number of questions and
concerns. The Administration had previously said that the Board would be
guided by, but not entirely bound to, the outcome of the performance
indicator review process; that Board members could apply discretion in their
selection. Performance trends, missing or old data, and recent policy actions
might come into play during selection deliberations, officials noted.

The final selection reflected decisions that both strictly followed the
performance indicator outcomes and applied Board discretion to take into
account other factors. Ten of the countries complied with the stated criteria:
performing above the median in relation to their peers on at least half of the
indicators in each of the three policy "baskets" and performing above the
median on corruption. The Board also examined whether a country
performed substantially below average on any single indicator and whether
their selection was supported by supplemental information. Each of the ten
countries also passed these additional tests.

For ten other countries, however, some discretion was applied by the
Board. In three cases, countries which met the criteria but fell significantly
below average on one indicator were still selected by the Board due to recent
policy changes or positive trend lines. Cape Verde, for example, scored

poorly on the Trade Policy indicator, but the Board took into account the country's progress towards joining the World Trade Organization and implementing a value added tax that will reduce reliance on import tariffs. Lesotho did not score well on the measurement for Days to Start a Business. The MCC Board, however, took note of Lesotho's creation of a central office to facilitate new business formation and saw positive performance on other factors related to business start-ups. Sri Lanka scored far below the median on Fiscal Policy, but the most recent trends suggested that the government was making progress in reducing its budget deficit.

For three other countries — Bolivia, Georgia, and Mozambique — the Board deviated from a strict application of the selection criteria because of evidence that the governments were taking corrective actions in the deficient areas. Bolivia fell at the median (as opposed to above the median) on the corruption indicator, something that would eliminate it from consideration. The Board, however, noted that President Mesa, who took office in October 2003, had created a cabinet position to coordinate anti-corruption activities and an office to investigate police corruption. Georgia, with a newly elected government that had created an anti-corruption bureau and taken other steps to fight corruption, was also selected despite scoring below the median on corruption and three other "ruling justly" indicators. Mozambique, which failed on corruption and each of the four "investing in people" indicators, was chosen based on supplemental data that was more current than information available from the primary data sources. This evidence, the Board felt, demonstrated Mozambique's commitment to fighting corruption and improving its performance on health and education.

On the other hand, the MCC Board chose not to select four countries that technically met the performance criteria but fell substantially below the median on one or more indicator. In each of these cases, the Board did not believe that the government was taking any action to improve its performance. Although Bhutan, Mauritania, and Vietnam passed the corruption hurdle and half of the "ruling justly" indicators, they scored very low on the measurements for Political Rights and Civil Liberties, and in Vietnam's case, on the Voice and Accountability indicator. A fourth country — Guyana — was also not selected despite passing the necessary hurdles. It scored particularly low on the Fiscal Policy measurement.[6]

It has been long assumed by MCC officials and close observers of the MCA initiative that when the country selections were announced, there would be disagreements and possible surprises in the final list, especially if the Board exercised its discretionary authority as it did for FY2004 participants. Representative Lowey, for example, expressed her view at a

May 13, 2004 House Appropriations Committee hearing that East Timor, which failed to pass the "economic freedom" hurdle in part due to missing data on two of the indicators, should have been selected. CEO Applegarth responded that East Timor is a new nation and that it was premature to conclude that it was a "high-performing" country. He acknowledged, however, that East Timor should be given close consideration in the future if the current trend lines continue.

Besides East Timor, some suggested that Kenya should have been included because of its new government's commitment to education and anti-corruption efforts. USAID Administrator Natsios acknowledged at the May 13 hearing that Albania was a "close call," failing because it scored slightly below the median on corruption. Like Albania, Malawi and Moldova would have qualified on the basis of performance if not for slightly failing scores on corruption. Several small island states, including Kiribati, Sao Tome, and Tonga, were not selected even though the absence of data for several categories may have played a role.[7]

Despite these questions over specific country eligibility, the selection process appeared to have satisfied two major concerns that have been consistently expressed over the past year. Based on earlier analysis, some argued that Africa would be under-represented in the final selection process, with perhaps as few as three regional states participating. In fact, eight, or half of the first year qualifying nations are from Africa.

Selection of countries that would give the appearance of geostrategic considerations was an additional concern of many who view the absence of security-related factors from MCA decision-making as one of the most attractive features of the initiative. For the most past, the Board appeared to have avoided this concern. Had the Board used its discretionary powers to select Indonesia, for example, some critics would have likely charged that the decision stemmed more from Jakarta's role in the war on terrorism than on strict policy performance. Indonesia passed all necessary hurdles except for corruption. Some, nevertheless, have questioned whether Georgia's selection was driven by broad U.S. foreign policy objectives of assisting a smooth political transition in the country rather than a choice based on performance.[8] Likewise, Bolivia, a country in which the United States maintains strong counter-narcotics goals, had been experiencing a period of instability despite strong performance prior to October 2003. Both Georgia and Bolivia were selected despite not strictly meeting the MCA performance criteria.

Naming Candidate Countries — FY2005

On July 20, 2004, the MCC Board of Directors launched the initial step in the FY2005 selection process by naming 70 candidate countries, 7 more than were reviewed for FY2004. After adjusting the per capita income upward to $1,465[9] and dropping the requirement that a country must be an IDA-eligible borrower from the World Bank, 11 new countries were added to the list: China, Egypt, Equatorial Guinea, Iraq, Morocco, Paraguay, Philippines, Swaziland, Turkmenistan, Tuvalu, and Ukraine. Four countries fell off the FY2005 list that had qualified in FY2004 —Albania, Bosnia and Herzegovina, Cape Verde, and Tonga — because their per capita income grew beyond the $1,465 cutoff. Thirteen other nations were excluded because they were ineligible for other U.S. economic assistance.[10]

Country Selection — FY2005

Meeting on November 8, the MCC Board of Directors made its selection of FY2005 eligible countries:

Armenia	Mali
Benin	Mongolia
Bolivia	Morocco
Georgia	Mozambique
Ghana	Nicaragua
Honduras	Senegal
Lesotho	Sri Lanka
Madagascar	Vanuatu

The Board chose one new country for FY2005 — Morocco — while 15 of the 16 nations included for FY2004 were determined eligible again for FY2005. Cape Verde was not selected due to the fact that its per capita GNI exceeded the $1,465 ceiling. Cape Verde, however, remains eligible for MCA support using FY2004 funds. Board selections represented both a high degree of continuity between FY2004 decisions as well as a sharp difference in the degree to which it applied its discretionary authority for qualifying or denying countries for FY2005.

Continuity in the FY2005 Selection Round

The fact that each country (except Cape Verde) selected for FY2004 MCA participation was also declared eligible for FY2005 should not be surprising, given the nature of the MCA concept. The Board identified in May 2004 what it determined to be the 16 "best performers" based on the assumption that these countries had, and would continue to express, a strong commitment to the types of economic, governance, and social policy reforms measured by the MCC. Absent a substantial negative development since May, there was a presumed expectation that these same countries would score well in a subsequent performance comparison with their income peers. Moreover, except in some extreme situations, evidence of a slide in policy performance as measured through the various data sources would likely lag behind the actual policy shift and not be reflected in the immediate data updates.

In addition, two other factors that may not apply in future years seem to have affected the outcome for FY2005. First, with the selection dates for FY2004 and FY2005 coming only six months apart — rather than one year, as should be the case in the future — it was likely that the data would indicate less change than might be the case if the comparisons occurred over a longer period. Between May and November, several of the data sources upon which the 16 performance indicators are based did not update or revise their figures.[11] As a result, the review of countries for FY2005 was based on much of the same data and rankings as had been the case for the FY2004 selection.

Moreover, the addition of 13 new countries for consideration in the FY2005 round had the effect for at least six of the indicators of lowering the median against which countries were compared. Because of this, if a country scored well — above the median — in the FY2004 selection decision, it was likely that it would score the same or better in the review for FY2005 where medians declined. For example, in May Bolivia fell exactly at the median on the corruption indicator. But in November, when the median for corruption dropped somewhat after new countries were added, Bolivia scored above the median even though Bolivia's score on corruption did not change. This phenomena is unlikely to be repeated again to the same extent since countries in the low-income group will be added or subtracted only if their economy grows beyond the per capita income ceiling or U.S. foreign aid sanctions are applied or lifted since the last review. The net effect is that the core set of low-income countries competing for MCA selection is unlikely to change as much as it did in FY2005, thereby reducing the extent to which the median will be altered simply because of the addition of new countries.

Excluding More Countries that Qualified

Despite the degree of continuity between FY2004 and FY2005 in the selection of eligible countries, the MCC Board departed somewhat from the previous round by not selecting a large number of countries that technically met the MCA performance criteria. Many observers raised questions over the FY2005 selections regarding the countries that were *not* selected rather than those that were.

As noted above, in May 2004, the Board chose not to select four countries —Bhutan, Guyana, Mauritania, and Vietnam — although each passed the minimum number of indicators. The Board decided to exclude these four because they scored "substantially below" the median on one or more measurements, although without defining precisely what represented a mark "substantially below"the median.

For FY2005, the Board did not select 10 countries that met the criteria, including three of the four left out of the FY2004 round (Mauritania did not meet the minimum qualifications). In addition, for FY2005 Burkina Faso, China, Djibouti, Egypt, Nepal, the Philippines, and Swaziland met the minimum standards but were not selected. The Corporation offered little explanation as to why these countries were not chosen.[12] It appears, however, that scoring "substantially below" — perhaps in the lowest 25th percentile — has become a de-facto criteria for exclusion. For example, the Corporation's CEO Paul Applegarth commented that the Philippines, a country that passed 13 of the 16 indicators, did not qualify because Manilla scored "substantially below" the median on tests for health expenditures and fiscal policy, and that more recent trends indicated the fiscal policy situation was deteriorating further.[13] Each of the other nine nations that met the minimum qualifications but were not selected also had one score in the 25th percentile, although the Corporation has not commented on whether this was the reason for not choosing them.

Another possible reason for limiting the number of qualifying countries in the FY2005 round might be due to funding reductions that were anticipated in early November. The Administration had requested combined FY2004/FY2005 appropriations of $3.8 billion, but was more likely, at the time of selection, to have available 25%-35% less, depending on the outcome of congressional debate on the FY2005 budget. Corporation officials have said that reduced funding would lead to fewer countries assisted and/or smaller grants per country, a situation that would be complicated further by qualifying additional nations.

Instead, the Board of Directors invited three of these 10 countries to participate in the Threshold Program, intended to help "near-miss" nations take steps to strengthen areas that would help them qualify for full MCA assistance in the future. Burkina Faso, Guyana, and the Philippines may now apply for Threshold Program assistance.

Another Board departure in the FY2005 selection process was to avoid using its discretionary authority to qualify countries that did not meet the minimum performance indicators. In May, the Board chose three nations — Bolivia, Georgia, and Mozambique — that did not pass the so-called "hard-hurdle" of corruption. The latter two again qualified despite falling below the median on corruption, while Bolivia did not require an exemption after the median dropped below its score with the addition of new countries. For FY2005, five nations — Malawi, Moldova, Paraguay, Tanzania, and Ukraine — passed the required number of performance indicators, except corruption. Although Malawi, Paraguay, and Tanzania are Threshold Countries, none of the five were chosen for full MCA status.

MCA Compacts and Program Proposals

The next step for qualified countries is the preparation and negotiation with the MCC of program proposals, referred to as MCA Compacts. Only those Compacts that demonstrate a strong relationship between the program proposal and economic growth and poverty reduction will receive funding. Not all qualified MCA countries may submit successful Compacts.

While acknowledging that Compact contents likely will vary, the Corporation expects each to discuss certain matters:

- a country's strategy for economic growth and poverty reduction, impediments to the strategy, how MCA aid will overcome the impediments, and the goals expected to be achieved during implementation of the Compact.;
- why the proposed program is a high priority for economic development and poverty reduction and why it will succeed; the process through which a public/private dialogue took place in developing the proposal;

- how the program will be managed, monitored, and sustained after the Compact expires;
- the relationship of other donor activities in the priority area;
- examples of projects, where appropriate;
- a multi-year financial plan; and
- a country's commitment to future progress on MCA performance indicators.

Madagascar and Honduras — The First MCA Compacts [14]

The Corporation did not set hard deadlines for Compact submissions in order to allow countries adequate time to conduct a national dialogue over the contents of the program proposal. As of December 1, 2004, the MCC had received proposals and "concept papers" from 15 of the 16 FY2004 eligible countries, and began the next phase — negotiating formal Compacts — with several countries. Meeting on March 14, 2005, the MCC Board of Directors announced the first Compact with Madagascar, an agreement that was signed on April 18. At the Board's meeting on May 20, a Compact with Honduras was approved, followed by its signing on June 13. MCC Board also approved two additional Compacts with Cape Verde and Nicaragua, and has notified Congress that Compact negotiations are underway with Georgia.

Madagascar Compact

The Madagascar Compact is a four year, $110 million program, focusing on rural agriculture development and poverty reduction. Specifically, the project has three objectives: 1) to increase land titling and land security ($36 million); 2) to expand the financial sector and increase competition ($36 million); and 3) to improve agricultural production technologies and market capacity in rural areas ($17 million). According to the Corporation's CEO, the Compact is designed to assist Madagascar's rural poor, which account for 80% of the nation's impoverished population, and generate income by expanding opportunities to own land, to access credit, and to gain technical training in agriculture and market identification.

Elements of the design, negotiation, and completion of the Madagascar Compact met several of the key criteria of the MCA process. For example, discussions regarding the scope and purpose of the MCA grant occurred at the regional and national level in Madagascar that included broad representation of civil society. Management and oversight of the Compact will be handled by a new entity, MCA-Madagascar, whose Steering Committee will include government and non-government officials. Both of these steps underscore the "country-ownership" and broad participatory nature of MCA programs. The Compact also includes fiscal accountability requirements concerning audits, monitoring, and evaluation that support the transparency concept of the MCA. While the $110 million MCA grant will be fully obligated when the Compact enters into force, resources will be transferred periodically following a determination that performance continues satisfactorily. This funding plan emphasizes the MCA principles of accountability and results. Other issues related to major MCA concepts and principles and how they are highlighted in the Madagascar program agreement will be examined once the complete text of the Compact is available following entry into force.

One matter, however, which has drawn the close attention of Congress and development policy analysts concerns the size of Madagascar's MCA grant. While Administration officials have said repeatedly that Compacts will be funded at various levels depending on the nature and potential impact of the proposal, the presumption has been that the MCA grant would represent a sizable increase in U.S. assistance to the eligible country. In order to realize its potential as a "transformational" aid program and to provide sufficient incentives to countries requesting "breakthrough" projects, the MCC says that the size of its grants must place MCA assistance among the top aid donors in a country.[15]

The four-year, $110 million Compact for Madagascar, however, does not appear to meet this criteria. USAID "core" economic aid programs in Madagascar have averaged about $20 million in recent years, with an additional supplement of $6 to $12 million in annual food aid. The $28 million per-year average of the MCA Compact will approximately double the level of U.S. assistance to Madagascar, assuming USAID maintains its program at current levels. But the MCA grant, it appears, will not be among the largest aid activities in Madagascar. France is the largest bilateral donor, providing on average $60 million, 2000-2002, a level that climbed substantially in 2003 to $142 million. The European Commission's aid program, 2001-2003, has averaged $63 million per year, while the World Bank's International Development Association is Madagascar's largest source of concessional assistance of about $170 million lent in each of 2002 and 2003.[16] The $110 million Compact for Madagascar is also not very large relative to the country's population. Of the 16 qualified countries for FY2004, Madagascar has the fourth largest population (16.4 million), and might have been expected to receive one of the larger MCA grants given its population size and its per capita income ($230, second lowest among the 16 MCA countries).

Honduras Compact

The five-year, $215 million MCA Compact with Honduras focuses on two objectives — rural development and transportation. The rural development project, representing $72.2 million of the Compact, will assist small and medium-size farmers enhance their business skills and to transition from the production of basic grains to horticultural crops, such as cucumbers, peppers, and tomatoes. According to CEO Applegarth, these vegetable crops will generate about $2,000 to $4,000 in annual income per hectare, compared with roughly $500 for basic grains. The project intends to provide farmers with the appropriate infrastructure and necessary training for producing and marketing these different crops. The transportation project, totaling $125.7 million of the Compact, will improve the major highway linking Honduran Atlantic and Pacific ports, and major production centers in Honduras, El Salvador, and Nicaragua. Rural roads will also be upgraded, helping farmers transport their goods to markets at a lower cost. Specific results sought in the Compact are:

- double productivity in 15,000 hectares in rural areas
- expand access to credit for farmers by over 20%
- upgrade the major road that links Honduras with commercial centers
- upgrade about 1,500 kilometers of rural roads

At nearly twice the size of the Madagascar Compact, the $215 million Honduras Compact will provide on average $43 million additional U.S. assistance over the five years of the program. By comparison, USAID development activities have averaged about $35 million the past two years, with $29 million requested for FY2006. U.S. disbursements of development assistance to Honduras, according to OECD sources, averaged over $100 million annually, 2000-2003. These higher levels reflect substantial assistance provided following the devastation of Hurricane Mitch in 1999. The United States has been Honduras' top aid donor in recent years, followed by Japan, the World Bank, and the Inter-American Development Bank.[17]

Table 1. Status of MCA Compacts

Country	Compact Signed	GNI per capita	Population Living Below $2 p/day (%)	Human Development Index Ranking[1]	FY05 US Econ. Aid (millions)	Compact Size (millions)	Compact Focus
Cape Verde	Pending	$1,440	NA	105	$1.7	$110 5 years	- Agriculture -Transportation/roads -Private Sector
Honduras	June 13, 2005	$970	44.0%	115	$22.6	$215 5 years	- Agriculture -Transportation/roads
Madagascar	April 18, 2005	$290	85.9%	150	$39.1	$110 four years	- Land titling - Financial sector - Agriculture
Nicaragua	Pending	$740	79.9%	118	$40.7	$175 five years	- Land titling -Transportation/roads - Agriculture

Sources: Population Living Below $2 Per Day — data from the World Bank, *World Development Indicators, 2005*; Gross National Income per capita — 2003 data from the World Bank, *World Development Indicators, 2005*. Human Development Index Rank — from UNDP, *Human Development Report, 2004*. U.S. Economic Aid — Department of State. MCA Compact information — Millennium Challenge Corporation.

1. The Human Development Index (HDI) is compiled by the U.N. Development Program and is published annually in the UNDP Human Development Report. It is a composite index that measures the average achievements in a country in three basic dimensions of human development: a long and healthy life, as measured by life expectancy at birth; knowledge, as measured by the adult literacy rate and the combined gross enrolment ratio for primary, secondary and tertiary schools; and a decent standard of living, as measured by GDP per capita in purchasing power parity (PPP) US dollars. The most recent report (2004) evaluates 171 countries, with number 1 having the best HDI and number 171 scoring the worst in the Index.

"Threshold" Countries and U.S. Assistance

In order to encourage non-qualifying countries to improve in weak areas, the United States will help governments that are committed to reform to strengthen performance so that they would be more competitive for MCA funding in future years. Congress provided in authorizing legislation that not more than 10% of MCA appropriations ($99.4 million in FY2004) could be used for such purposes, stating that the funding could be made available through USAID. The MCC set aside up to $40 million for countries that just missed qualifying for FY2004 funding and projects an additional $90 million for FY2005, subject To the quality of submitted proposals.[18]

The Corporation has made two announcements regarding the selection of Threshold Countries. On September 30, the Corporation named seven participants: Albania, East Timor, Kenya, Sao Tome and Principe, Tanzania, Uganda, and Yemen. Five weeks later, on November 8, the MCC added six more nations for FY2005: Burkina Faso, Guyana, Malawi, Paraguay, the Philippines, and Zambia. According to the Threshold Program Policy guidance issued by the Corporation,[19] the program will assist countries make policy reforms and institutional changes in areas where they failed to meet the MCA performance criteria. In order to qualify for Threshold Program FY2004 assistance, countries must have submitted by January 31, 2005, concept papers identifying:

- where and why the country failed to pass specific indicators;
- proposals for policy, regulatory, or institutional reforms that would improve the country's performance on these indicators; and
- types of assistance, over a two-year maximum period, required to implement these reforms.

If the Corporation, in consultation with USAID, determines that the concept paper shows sufficient commitment to reform and a promise of success, the country will prepare a Threshold Country Plan that specifically establishes a program schedule, the means to measure progress, and financing requirements, among other considerations. USAID is charged with overseeing the implementation of Threshold Country Plans, including working with countries to identify appropriate implementing partners such as local, U.S., and international firms; NGOs; U.S. government agencies; and international organizations. Like regular MCA Compacts, funding is not guaranteed for each country selected for the Threshold Program, but will be based on the quality of the Country Plan.

Role of USAID and the Future of Agency Programs in MCA Countries

As noted above, how USAID would participate in the MCA initiative has been a continuing concern of Congress and various policy analysts. Legislation authorizing the MCC requires the Corporation's CEO to coordinate with USAID and directs the Agency to ensure that its programs play a primary role in helping candidate countries prepare for MCA consideration. Corporation and USAID officials have said there will be close collaboration between the two entities, although the precise nature of the relationship has yet to be made public. USAID maintains missions in 14 of the 17 eligible countries and might be expected to support MCC programs, through contracting, procurement, and monitoring tasks.

Another question is how USAID will adjust its own programs in MCA countries, especially where the Agency maintains relatively small activities in relation to other donors. Since the goal is to provide resources that will make MCA programs among the largest aid operations in a country, it was anticipated that USAID spending would fall well below amounts provided through MCC Compacts. For example, in Mongolia, where U.S. aid programs have totaled $10-$12 million annually in recent years, the United States was the fourth largest bilateral donor in 2002, representing less than a quarter of the size of Japan's economic aid disbursements. In Ghana, Senegal, and Sri Lanka, USAID maintains larger programs but spends far less than other countries and multilateral agencies. But in the case of the first Compacts for Madagascar and Honduras, the MCA grants are only somewhat higher on a per-year average ($28 million for Madagascar and $43 million for Honduras) than USAID's "core" economic aid programs (about $20 million for Madagascar and $34 million for Honduras).

Like other issues involving USAID, this question remains under review. USAID Administrator Natsios told the House Appropriations Committee on May 9, 2004 that the Agency would not withdraw from or cut programs in MCA countries, but would not increase spending either. He said, however, that USAID would work to ensure that its programs operate in an integrated way with MCA-funded activities.

The first test will come in Madagascar where the MCA Compact focuses on rural agriculture, land tenure, and the financial sector, with an anticipated outcome of protecting the country's fragile ecosystem. USAID's current program is largely targeted on preventing sexually transmitted infections and HIV/AIDS, strengthening health services, improving the nation's governance capacity, conserving Madagascar's biologically diverse forest ecosystems, and promoting agriculture market development and trade. The latter two objectives appear to be consistent with the MCA Compact. Adjustments to USAID's program could be made in the future, however, as the Agency undertakes a review of its strategic goals now that Madagascar entered into an MCA program.

Funding Issues — Previous and in the 109th Congress

As mentioned above, Congress appropriated $994 million for FY2004 MCC programs and an additional $1.488 billion for FY2005. The enacted appropriation for FY2005 is 40% below the President's $2.5 billion request. The MCC recommendation was by far the largest increase sought by the Administration in the Foreign Operations appropriations proposal and viewed by many observers as one of the most vulnerable items in an increasingly difficult budget environment. In earlier congressional action, House and Senate Budget Committees (H.Con.Res. 393 and S.Con.Res. 95) recommended reductions in international affairs spending, suggesting that much of the proposed cuts could be achieved by trimming back the MCC request. Legislation authorizing appropriations for the MCC reported by the Senate Foreign Relations Committee (S. 2144) would have reduced the level to $2 billion.

Foreign Operations appropriation bills passed in both the House and Senate (H.R. 4818) made substantial reductions to the President's MCC request for FY2005. The bill, as approved by the House, reduced by half the President's $2.5 billion proposal. In cutting the MCC proposal, the House Appropriations Committee noted that its decision resulted solely from the constrained budget environment in FY2005 and the need to address other Administration and Congressional priorities. The executive branch, in its Statement of Administration Policy on H.R. 4818, expressed its "disappointment" over the level of MCC funding and urged Congress to increase resources. During floor debate on July 15, the House defeated (41-379) an amendment by Representative Paul to eliminate all MCC appropriations.

The House Committee, in its report on H.R. 4818, also expressed concern over Corporation plans to enter into multi-year Compacts without committing total funding for these programs in the year the Compact is signed. This, the Committee believed, would obligate future Congresses to fund prior year contracts. Consequently, the bill required the MCC to only sign Compacts for which complete funding was available from existing appropriations. The House Committee also recommended that Compacts be limited to a 3-4 year period rather than a 3-5 year duration envisioned by the MCC.

The Senate measure — also H.R. 4818, as amended to incorporate the text of S. 2812, proposed a more significant cut to the President's MCC request — to $1.12 billion. Despite the reduction, the Senate Appropriations Committee noted its strong support for the program.

Following strong pressure from the White House to increase MCC funding above House and Senate-passed levels, conferees settled on $1.5 billion for the MCC in FY2005, adjusted downward to $1.488 billion by an across-the-board rescission requirement. Like the House bill, the conference agreement requires that the MCC fully fund multi-year compacts selected in FY2004 and FY2005.

For some time, some Members of Congress have raised questions regarding whether sufficient funds will be available to support MCC programs in every country selected, especially if the Board continues its practice of selecting more countries than meet the strict criteria. Representative Kolbe, chairman of the House Foreign Operations Subcommittee, speculated at a May 9, 2004, hearing that based on recent Board decisions, by 2006, as many as 40 countries might have qualified. This, he believed, could not be fully supported with likely funding levels, and might raise country expectations that could not be met and undermine program incentives.

MCC officials point out that qualification for the program does not mean that a government will receive funding. That decision will be based on the quality of the Compact proposals and it is possible that the Corporation will not finalize agreements with all eligible countries. Nevertheless, the Corporation's CEO Paul Applegarth acknowledged the funding dilemma for future MCC operations at a Senate Foreign Relations Committee hearing on October 5, noting that the sum of proposals received thus far totaled $4.2 billion.

A March 2004 GAO report estimated that the MCC could adequately fund 8-13 Compacts with an appropriation of $3.5 billion (the combined FY2004 enacted and FY2005 requested amounts). This suggests, that even if Congress had fully funded the FY2005 proposal, the Corporation would not be able to support programs in all 17 countries approved for FY2004 and FY2005. With $1 billion less than the assumption used by GAO in its assessment, the MCC may face increasing difficulties funding Compacts of a sufficient size that will have a meaningful impact on a country's economic growth and poverty reduction goals. This may lead to further congressional examination of the Board's selection process and consideration of ways to limit the number of countries selected in the future.

MCA Request for FY2006

The Administration seeks a $3 billion appropriation for FY2006, a level that has been criticized for being both too small and too large. Some argue that given the heightened budget pressures and proposed reductions for many domestic programs, coupled with the fact that the MCC has spent only $4 million of the nearly $2.5 billion in existing appropriations, a request for roughly double the amount provided in FY2005 is not warranted. Others, however, note that President Bush pledged an MCA funding level of $5 billion by FY2006 when he announced the initiative in March 2002, and believe the Administration should stick with its promise regardless of congressional reductions the past two years. The MCC calls its $3 billion budget proposal a realistic level given prior congressional actions and competing resource demands.

Countering the argument that the Corporation has spent only a fraction of its resources, MCC officials say that program proposals received thus far total more than $3 billion, not including Morocco (the largest eligible country), and will exhaust available resources by early 2006. The Corporation, in its FY2006 budget justification to Congress, estimates that it will sign 18 Compacts with low-income countries using FY2004-FY2006 funds, totaling just over $4 billion, or an average Compact size of nearly $225 million. The MCC budget assumptions also include four new Compacts in FY2006 with low-middle income countries which become eligible in FY2006 to compete for MCA grants. These costs would add $680 million or an average of $170 million per Compact. The remaining $800 million would be divided among amendments to earlier Compacts ($300 million), Threshold country programs ($270 million), and administrative and related expenses (over $200 million).

These MCA budget projections appear to assume that all, or nearly all eligible low-income countries will sign Compacts, and that four of the roughly 30 new low-middle income nations will reach an MCA agreement by the end of FY2006. If so, MCA financed programs could absorb the total $4.7 billion budgeted for Compacts, FY2004-2006, but only if subsequent Compacts are of the size of the Honduras Compact and significantly larger in dollar terms than the Madagascar program. Another outcome that could place fiscal constraints on the MCC is if a substantial number of new low income countries are selected for FY2006. Based on previous experience and assumptions set out in the Corporation's FY2006 budget justification, this scenario is unlikely.

Implications for the FY2007 budget are also unclear. Because a country must complete one MCA program before applying for a second, none of the 22 potential Compact countries assumed in the MCC budget documents would be eligible for a subsequent grant until FY2008. Given that only one new country was added to the eligible list in FY2005, and that the MCC projects another five in FY2006, a possible FY2007 funding level of between $3 and $5 billion would suggest several possible scenarios: a surge (unlike FY2005 and FY2006) in the number of newly eligible countries, possibly including the elevation of Threshold countries to full MCA eligible status; significant amendments to existing Compacts increasing their size; or the creation of a large funding reserve that could be utilized in subsequent years as current MCA countries complete programs and apply for new grants.

Congressional Action

In the first legislative action on the FY2006 MCA request, the Senate Foreign Relations Committee, in S. 600, authorizes $3 billion, as proposed, and such sums as may be necessary for FY2007.

The House, however, voted on June 28 to reduce the FY2006 MCA funding level to $1.75 billion (H.R. 3057). The Appropriation Committee's report on the legislation said that the reduction stemmed solely from the constrained budget environment and the need to allocate resources to other Presidential and congressional priorities. In order to operate in FY2006 with reduced resources, the Committee recommended that the Corporation not use funds for amending and increasing existing Compacts, but to maximize the number of new compacts with available appropriations.

The Senate Appropriations Committee recommended on June 30 (also H.R. 3057) a slightly higher MCA appropriation, providing $1.8 billion. The Committee, in its report (H.Rept. 109-96), also said that the constrained budget allocation was one reason for the reduced appropriation. The Senate panel, however, further noted that the MCC had obligated less than $34 million of the nearly $2.5 billion in existing funds, and that the average value to the two signed Compacts was about one-half of what the Corporation stated in its budget justification. The Committee further expressed concern about coordination and consistency with other U.S. aid programs in MCA countries, and directed the Secretary of State to report on these issues, including an assessment of whether MCA programs were duplicative of USAID or other aid activities in Compact countries.

Table 2. MCA Candidate, Eligible, and Threshold Countries — FY2004

Africa	Income*	East Asia/Pacific	Income*	Latin America	Income*
Angola	$660	East Timor (TC)	$430	**Bolivia**	$940
Benin	$390	Indonesia	$680	Guyana	$840
Burkina Faso	$220	Kiribati	$810	Haiti	$440
Cameroon	$560	Laos	$310	**Honduras**	$920
Cape Verde	$1,290	**Mongolia**	$440	**Nicaragua**	**
Chad	$220	Papua New Guinea	$580		
Comoros	$390	Solomon Islands	$570		
Congo, Dem Rep of	$90	Tonga	$1,410		
Congo, Rep of	$700	**Vanuatu**	$1,080		
Eritrea	$160	Vietnam	$430		
Ethiopia	$100				
Gambia	$280	**South Asia**	**Income***	**Mid-East**	**Income***
Ghana	$270	Afghanistan	**	Djibouti	$900
Guinea	$410	Bangladesh	$360	Yemen (TC)	$490
Kenya (TC)	$360	Bhutan	$590		
Lesotho	$470	India	$460		
Madagascar	$240	Nepal	$230		
Malawi	$160	Pakistan	$420		
Mali	$240	**Sri Lanka**	$840		
Mauritania	$340				
Mozambique	$210	**Eurasia**	**Income***	**Europe**	**Income***
Niger	$170	**Armenia**	$790	Albania(TC)	$1,380
Nigeria	$290	Azerbaijan	$650	Bosnia	$1,270
Rwanda	$230	**Georgia**	$720		
Sao Tome and Principe (TC)	$290	Kyrgyz Rep.	$290		
Senegal	$470	Moldova	$460		
Sierra Leone	$140	Tajikistan	$180		
Tanzania (TC)	$280				
Togo	$270				
Uganda (TC)	$240				
Zambia	$330				

* Gross National Income, dollars per capita, 2002. *World Bank Annual Report, 2003.*
** Precise data unavailable.

Notes: **Criteria**: IDA-eligible, per capita income $1,415 and below, and not prohibited from receiving other U.S. economic assistance.
Eligible Countries are in Bold.
Threshold Countries are followed with (TC)

Table 3. MCA Candidate, Eligible, and Threshold Countries — FY2005

Africa	Income*	East Asia/Pacific	Income*	Latin America	Income*
Angola	$740	China	$1,100	**Bolivia**	$890
Benin	$440	East Timor (TC)	$430	Guyana(TC)	$900
Burkina Faso (TC)	$300	Indonesia	$810	Haiti	$380
Cameroon	$640	Kiribati	$880	**Honduras**	$970
Chad	$250	Laos	$320	**Nicaragua**	$730
Comoros	$450	**Mongolia**	$480	Paraguay(TC	$1,100
Congo, Dem Rep	$100	Papua New Guinea	$510		
Congo, Rep of	$640	Philippines (TC)	$1,080		
Equatorial Guinea	**	Solomon Islands	$600		
Eritrea	$190	Tuvalu	**		
Ethiopia	$90	**Vanuatu**	$1,180		
Gambia	$310	Vietnam	$480		
Ghana	$320				
Guinea	$430	**South Asia**	**Income***	**Mid-East**	**Income***
Kenya (TC)	$390	Afghanistan	**	Djibouti	$910
Lesotho	$590	Bangladesh	$400	Egypt	$1,390
Madagascar	$290	Bhutan	$660	Iraq	**
Malawi (TC)	$170	India	$530	**Morocco**	$1,320
Mali	$290	Nepal	$240	Yemen (TC)	$520
Mauritania	$430	Pakistan	$470		
Mozambique	$210	**Sri Lanka**	$930		
Niger	$200				
Nigeria	$320	**Eurasia**	**Income***	**Europe**	**Income***
Rwanda	$220	**Armenia**	$950		
Sao Tome and Principe (TC)	$320	Azerbaijan	$810		
Senegal	$550	**Georgia**	$830		
Sierra Leone	$150	Kyrgyz Rep.	$330		
Swaziland	$1,350	Moldova	$590		
Tanzania (TC)	$290	Tajikistan	$190		
Togo	$310	Turkmenistan	$1,120		
Uganda (TC)	$240	Ukraine	$970		
Zambia (TC)	$380				

* Gross National Income, dollars per capita, 2003. *World Bank Annual Report, 2004.*
** Precise data unavailable.

Notes: **Criteria:** Per capita income $1,465 and below, and not prohibited from receiving other U.S. economic assistance.
Eligible Countries are in Bold.
Threshold Countries are followed with (TC)

Table 4. MCA Potential Candidate Countries — FY2006

Africa	Income*	East Asia/Pacific	Income*	Latin America	Income*
Angola	$740	East Timor	$430	Belize	**
Benin	$440	Fiji	$2,360	Bolivia	$890
Burkina Faso	$300	Indonesia	$810	Brazil	$2,710
Cameroon	$640	Kiribati	$880	Colombia	$1,810
Cape Verde	$1,490	Laos	$320	Dominican Rep	$2,070
Chad	$250	Marshall Islands	$2,710	Ecuador	$1,790
Comoros	$450	Micronesia	$2,090	El Salvador	$2,200
Congo, Dem Rep of	$100	Mongolia	$480	Guatemala	$1,910
Congo, Rep of	$640	Papua New Guinea	$510	Guyana	$900
Equatorial Guinea	**	Philippines	$1,080	Haiti	$380
Eritrea	$190	Samoa	$1,600	Honduras	$970
Ethiopia	$90	Solomon Islands	$600	Jamaica	$2,760
Gambia	$310	Thailand	$2,190	Nicaragua	$730
Ghana	$320	Tonga	$1,460	Paraguay	$1,100
Guinea	$430	Tuvalu	**	Peru	$2,150
Kenya	$390	Vanuatu	$1,180	Suriname	**
Lesotho	$590	Vietnam	$480		
Madagascar	$290				
Malawi	$170	**South Asia**	**Income***	**Mid-East**	**Income***
Mali	$290	Afghanistan	**	Algeria	$1,890
Mauritania	$430	Bangladesh	$400	Djibouti	$910
Mozambique	$210	Bhutan	$660	Egypt	$1,390
Namibia	$1,870	India	$530	Iraq	**
Niger	$200	Nepal	$240	Jordan	$1,850
Nigeria	$320	Pakistan	$470	Morocco	$1,320
Rwanda	$220	Sri Lanka	$930	Tunisia	$2,240
Sao Tome and Principe	$320			Yemen	$520
Senegal	$550	**Eurasia**	**Income***		
Sierra Leone	$150	Armenia	$950	**Europe**	**Income***
South Africa	$2,780	Azerbaijan	$810	Albania	$1,740
Swaziland	$1,350	Belarus	$1,590	Bulgaria	$2,130
Tanzania	$290	Georgia	$830	Bosnia	$1,540
Togo	$310	Kazakhstan	$1,780	Macedonia	$1,980
Uganda	$240	Kyrgyz Rep.	$330	Romania	$2,310
Zambia	$380	Moldova	$590	Turkey	$2,790
		Russia	$2,610		
		Tajikistan	$190		
		Turkmenistan	$1,120		
		Ukraine	$970		

* Gross National Income, dollars per capita, 2003. *World Bank Annual Report, 2004.*
** Precise data unavailable.

Notes: **Criteria**: Per capita income $3,035 and below, and not prohibited from receiving other U.S. economic assistance.[20]

Table 5. MCC Performance Indicators for FY2005

Ruling Justly	Investing in People	Economic Freedom
Control of Corruption Source: World Bank Institute [http://www.worldbank.org/wbi/governance/govdat a2002/index.html]	**Public Primary Education Spending as % of GDP** Sources: National governments	**Country Credit Rating** Source: Institutional Investor Magazine, September 2004.
Voice and Accountability Source: World Bank Institute [http://www.worldbank.org/wbi/governance/govdat a2002/index.html]	**Primary Girls' Education Completion Rate** Sources: World Bank and UNESCO	**Inflation** (must be below 15%) Source: Multiple
Government Effectiveness Source: World Bank Institute [http://www.worldbank.org/wbi/governance/govdat a2002/index.html]	**Public Expenditure on Health as % of GDP** Sources: National governments	**Fiscal Policy** Source: National governments and IMF World Economic Outlook
Rule of Law Source: World Bank Institute [http://www.worldbank.org/wbi/governance/govdat a2002/index.html]	**Immunization Rates: DPT and Measles** Sources: World Health Organization	**Trade Policy** Source: The Heritage Foundation, Index of Economic Freecom http://www.heritage.org/research/ features/index/]
Civil Liberties Source: Freedom House [http://www.freedomhouse.org/research/freeworld/ 2004/table2004.pdf]		**Regulatory Policy** Source: World Bank Institrte [http://www.worldbank.org/wbi/ governance/govdat a2002/index.html]
Political Freedom Source: Freedom House[http://www.freedomhouse.org/research/freeworld/ 2004/table2004.pdf]		**Days to Start a Business** Source: World Bank[http://rru.worldbank.org/ DoingBusiness/Explore Topics/StartingBusiness/ CompareAll.aspx]

Table 6. Comparison of MCA Authorization Legislation

Issue	Administration	Senate (S. 925)[a]	House (H.R. 1950)[a]	Conference (H.R. 2673)
MCA oversight	Board of Directors, chaired by Sec. of State, with Treasury and OMB	Board of Directors, chaired by the Sec. of State, with Treasury, USAID, USTR, and the MCA's Chief Executive Officer (CEO)	Board of Directors, chaired by Sec. of State, with Treasury, USTR, USAID, MCC CEO, and 4 others nominated by the President from a Congressional list. Non-voting members include OPIC, OMB, Peace Corps, and TDA.	Board of Directors, chaired by Sec. of State, with Treasury, USTR, USAID, MCC CEO, and 4 others nominated by the President that may come from list submitted by Congressional leaders.
MCA organization	Independent Millennium Challenge Corporation	Independent Millennium Challenge Corporation whose CEO reports to and be under the direct authority and foreign policy guidance of the Sec. of State	Independent Millennium Challenge Corporation	Independent Millennium Challenge Corporation
MCA coordinator	CEO of Corporation	CEO "manages" the Corporation, reporting to and under the direct authority and foreign policy guidance of the Sec. of State	CEO "heads" the Corporation, reporting to the President	CEO "manages" the Corporation, reporting to and under the direct authority and foreign policy guidance of the Board of Directors.
Interim CEO	—	—	—	Board of Directors may appoint a confirmed U.S. Government official to serve as interim CEO until a CEO has been confirmed by the Senate.
Selection of countries	Board of Directors	Board of Directors	CEO of Corporation	Board of Directors

Table 6. Comparison of MCA Authorization Legislation (cont.)

MCC Advisory Council	None	None	Nine members named by the CEO to advise on MCA policy, review eligibility criteria, evaluate the MCC, assess MCC capabilities, and make recommendations to the CEO.	None
Country income eligibility	FY2004 - IDA eligible and per capita GNI less than historical IDA level for the year ($1,415 in FY2004) FY2005 - per capita GNI less than historical IDA level for the year ($1,465 in FY2005) FY2006 - per capita GNI less than historical IDA level for the year ($1,465 in FY2005), plus low-middle income countries as defined in the World Bank Development Report ($3,035 in FY2005)	FY2004 - IDA eligible FY2005 - per capita GNI less than historical IDA cutoff for the year ($1,465 in FY2005) FY2006 - per capita GNI less than historical IDA cutoff for the year ($1,465 in FY2005), plus, if appropriation exceeds $5 billion, low-middle income countries as defined in the World Bank Development Report ($3,035 in FY2005); low-middle income countries capped at 20%	FY2004 - IDA eligible and per capita GNI less than historical IDA level for the year ($1,415 in FY2004) FY2005 - per capita GNI less than historical IDA level for the year ($1,465 in FY2005) FY2006 - per capita GNI less than historical IDA level for the year ($1,465 in FY2005), plus low-middle income countries as defined in the World Bank Development Report ($3,035 in FY2005); low-middle income countries capped at 20%	FY2004 - IDA eligible and per capita GNI less than historical IDA level for the year ($1,415 in FY2004) FY2005 - per capita GNI less than historical IDA level for the year ($1,465 in FY2005) FY2006 - per capita GNI less than historical IDA level for the year ($1,465 in FY2005), plus low-middle income countries as defined in the World Bank Development Report ($3,035 in FY2005); low-middle income countries capped at 25%
Eligible entity	None stated	A government, including a local or regional government, or an NGO or private entity.	A national government, regional or local government, an NGO, an international organization and trust funcs.	A national government, regional or local government, or an NGO or private entity.

Table 6. Comparison of MCA Authorization Legislation (cont.)

Aid to "threshold" countries	General support	10% of MCA funds available for countries failing to qualify because of inadequate data or missing one indicator	15% of MCA funds available for countries demonstrating a development commitment but fail to meet a sufficient number of performance indicators	10% of MCA funds available for countries showing a commitment to MCA criteria but fail to qualify
Oversight and reports	MCA contracts and performance posted on the Internet.	Disclosure in Federal Register and on the Internet of eligible countries, programs supported, and performance; proposed performance indicators open to public comment; annual report to Congress	CEO consultation with Congress on eligibility criteria; notification 15 days in advance on grants exceeding $5 million; "Compacts" with countries published in Federal Register and on the Internet; advance notification of aid termination; annual reports to Congress from the CEO and Advisory Council	Establishes a period of at least 95 days during which Congress will receive the list of "candidate countries," the eligibility criteria and methodology for making a final selection, and the list of "eligible" countries (those that will receive MCA assistance). Consultation with congressional committees will occur during this period and the information will be published in the Federal Register. "Compacts" with countries will be reported to Congress and published in Federal Register.

Table 6. Comparison of MCA Authorization Legislation (cont.)

Funding	FY2004 - $1.3 billion FY2005 - no decision FY2006 - $5 billion	FY2004 - $1 billion FY2005 - $2.3 billion FY2006 - $5 billion	FY2004 - $1.3 billion FY2005 - $3 billion FY2006 - $5 billion	Such sums as may be necessary for FY2004 and FY2005.

a. The Senate position is based on S. 925, the Foreign Affairs Act, Fiscal Year 2004, as amended, but not passed during debate on July 9 and 10, 2003. The House position is taken from H.R. 1950, an omnibus foreign policy authorization measure which passed the House on July 16, 2003.

ENDNOTES

[1] For a more in-depth discussion of the original MCA proposal and issues debated by Congress in 2003, see CRS Report RL31687, *The Millennium Challenge Account: Congressional Consideration of a New Foreign Aid Initiative.*

[2] **Table 2**, found at the end of this report, provides a summary of major MCA issues and compares positions approved by the House, Senate, and Conference Committee during the 2003 debate.

[3] On July 13, 2004, the Senate confirmed two of the four new Board members: Kenneth Hackett, President and CEO of Catholic Relief Services, and Christine Todd Whitman, former Governor of New Jersey and former head of the Environmental Protection Agency, 2001-2003. No further nominees have been submitted by the White House.

[4] Various types of aid restrictions applied to these countries. For several — Burundi, Central African Republic, Cote d'Ivoire, Guinea-Bissau, and Sudan — U.S. aid was blocked because an elected head of government had been deposed by a military coup. For Cambodia and Uzbekistan, legislation banned FY2004 assistance to the central governments of these countries. Aid restrictions imposed on nations not cooperating in counter-narcotics efforts (Burma), that are on the terrorist list (Sudan), or in arrears on debt owed the United States (Liberia, Somalia, and Zimbabwe) also applied. Serbia could not receive aid in FY2004 unless the President issued a determination stating, among other things, that the government was cooperating with the International Criminal Tribunal. Notwithstanding these restrictions, each country remained eligible for humanitarian assistance from the United States.

[5] See, for example, Steve Radelet, et al., *A Comment on the Millennium Challenge Account Selection Process*, Center for Global Development, March 9, 2004.

[6] For a complete statement regarding the Board's rationale, see *Report on the Selection of MCA Eligible Countries for FY2004,* found at [http://www.mcc.gov], "Congressional Reports."

[7] As noted below, East Timor, Albania, and Sao Tome were subsequently selected as three of the seven "threshold" countries that will receive assistance to help the country meet the MCA requirements.

[8] See Steve Radelet, *A Note on the MCC Selection Process for 2005*, September 23, 2004, found at [http://www.cgdev.org].

[9] The MCC plans to adjust the per capita income threshold each year to correspond to the per capita income cutoff of the "historic ceiling" of IDA lending, a calculation made by the World Bank. In future years when all lower-middle income countries will be eligible to compete,

the MCC also will adjust that threshold — which grew from $2,975 in 2003 to $3,035 in 2004 — in the consideration of determining candidate countries.

[10] Eleven of these countries were also excluded in FY2004. Serbia, which was barred from consideration for FY2004, exceeded the per capita income limit for FY2005 so was not under consideration. Syria and Cuba, which became potential candidate countries beginning in FY2005, were excluded because of a ban on direct aid to the countries. See Footnote 4, above, for a complete list of countries and aid restrictions.

[11] This is not true for the performance indicators of Inflation and Primary Girls Graduation Rate, which were modified for the FY2005 selection, or for the indicators measuring Days to Start a Business, Civil Liberties, and Political Freedom which were updated in 2004. For some of the other economic and social investment indicators where data were drawn from national sources, revised figures were used in the FY2005 selection, but only where available. World Bank data for six governance-related indicators and the Trade Policy measurement, however, were not revised between May and November 2004.

[12] The MCC's authorizing legislation (section 608(d)) requires the Corporation's CEO to provide justification to Congress regarding only those countries declared as eligible for MCA assistance and for those selected for Compact negotiation. Otherwise, there is no statutory requirement for the MCC to comment on its decision-making process, including the rationale for not selecting specific countries.

[13] Comments by Paul Applegarth at a State Department Foreign Press Center Briefing, November 9, 2004.

[14] Details of the Madagascar and Honduras Compacts can be found at the MCA website: [http://www.mcc.gov]. Specific information on Madagascar is available at [http://www.mcc.gov/compacts/madagascar.shtml].

[15] See, for example, Millennium Challenge Corporation FY2005 Budget Justification, p. 7. Found at [http://www.mcc.gov/about_us/key_documents/index.shtml].

[16] Organization for Economic Cooperation and Development, *Geographical Distribution of Financial Flows to Aid Recipients, 1999/2003: 2005 edition.* p. 172.

[17] OECD. *Geographical Distribution of Financial Flows to Aid Recipients, 1999-2003*, p. 152.

[18] Initially, assistance for Threshold countries was authorized only for FY2004. The FY2005 Foreign Operations Appropriations (Division D of P.L. 108-447, the Consolidated Appropriations Act for FY2005, makes 10%, or $149 million of the new appropriation available Threshold assistance.

[19] Found at [http://www.MCC.gov].
[20] The $3,035 per capita GNI figure would be the ceiling for FY2005 but
      will be adjusted in July 2005 when the World Bank releases a new
      World Development Report. It is likely that the per capita GNI ceiling
      for lower-middle income countries will rise somewhat, but at this time,
      it is impossible to say what that level might be or precisely identify
      which countries will fall under the ceiling. This list is an estimate based
      on the current lower-middle income ceiling and those countries that are
      currently defined by the World Bank as lower-middle income and are
      not prohibited from receiving U.S. economic assistance.

In: Foreign Aid: Control, Corrupt, Contain?   ISBN 1-60021-067-8
Editor: A. A. Bealinger, pp. 101-108   © 2006 Nova Science Publishers, Inc.

Chapter 4

INTERNATIONAL FOOD AID: U.S. AND OTHER DONOR CONTRIBUTIONS[*]

Charles E. Hanrahan and Carol Canada

ABSTRACT

The United States is the world's major provider of international food aid to low-income developing countries. This report provides three indicators of the U.S. contribution to global food aid: (1) shipments of major donors compiled by the International Grains Council, (2) U.S. contributions to the United Nations World Food Program (WFP), and (3) the U.S. commitment under the Food Aid Convention (FAC).

U.S. food aid accounted for 59% of food aid shipments by major donors during 1995-2003. A substantial portion of U.S. food aid is channeled through the WFP. During 1996-2004, around 48% of the food aid distributed by the WFP came from the United States. The Food Aid Convention (FAC), now expired, was an agreement among donor countries to provide a minimum amount of food aid to low-income developing countries. The food aid commitment by all FAC signatories was approximately 4.9 million metric tons (mmt). The United States pledged to provide 2.5 mmt or 51% of the total commitment.

---

[*] Excerpted from CRS Report RS21279, dated May 2, 2005.

CONTRIBUTIONS OF MAJOR DONORS TO
INTERNATIONAL FOOD AID

The United States is the major contributor to international food aid, supplying on average, since 1995, around 59% of annual total food aid (see Figure 1) provided by donors who are members of the Food Aid Committee of the International Grains Council and signatories of the 1999 Food Aid Convention.[1] U.S. contributions increased from around 2.8 million metric tons (mmt) measured in wheat equivalent in 1995/ 1996 to about 6.1 mmt in 2002/2003 (see Appendix Table 1).[2] U.S. contributions averaged 4.8 mmt annually. Food aid from the European Union (including food aid provided by the European Commission and by individual member countries of the EU) has been more stable and averaged around 2.1 mmt or 26% of average annual food aid shipments. Japan and Canada provided 5.7% and 5.2%, respectively, of the total from major donors. Japan's contributions are provided as cash rather than commodities.

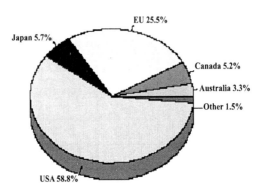

Figure 1. Food Aid by Major Donors, 1995-2003

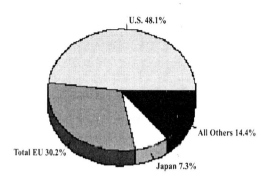

* Data as of April 11, 2005.
Figure 2. Food Aid Contributions to the World Food Programme, 1996-2005.*

Because food aid data are reported on a July/ June marketing year basis, they do not correspond, for example, to fiscal year food aid data reported by the U.S. Department of Agriculture in   budget documents or by the U.S. Agency for International Development in annual food aid reports. The source of the data in Figure 1 and Appendix Table 1 is the annual report *Food Aid Shipments*, prepared by the Food Aid Committee of the International Grains Council.[3]

FOOD AID CONTRIBUTIONS TO THE WORLD FOOD PROGRAM

Most U.S. food aid is provided on a bilateral basis, but a substantial portion is channeled through the United Nations World Food Program (WFP), the intergovernmental agency that provides food aid for development projects and humanitarian relief in low income countries. More than 56 donors, mainly countries, but also some non-governmental organizations like the International Red Cross, contribute to the WFP. The United States is the major donor, providing over the last nine years around 48% of total WFP contributions (see Figure 2 and Appendix Table 2). Over that same nine-year period, the EU (again combining European Commission with EU member countries' contributions) accounted for around 30% of total WFP contributions. Japan, whose contributions are in cash, provided around 7%. The remaining donors combined provided about 14% to WFP food aid resources. Donor contributions to the WFP are not in addition to, but are included in, the data reported in Figure 1 and Appendix Table 1.

COMMITMENTS UNDER THE FOOD AID CONVENTION

The Food Aid Convention (FAC), first agreed to in 1968 during the Kennedy Round multilateral trade negotiations held under the auspices of the General Agreements on Tariffs and Trade (GATT), was an international agreement that constituted a framework of cooperation on food aid Figure 3. Food Aid Commitments between major donors. The food aid commitment under the under the Food Aid Convention, 1999 FAC was a minimum commitment and was intended to be a guarantee of food security for low-income developing countries. The signatories of the FAC were Argentina, Australia, Canada, the European Union and its member countries, Japan, Norway, Switzerland, and the United States. Signatories could provide more than their minimum commitment. The current FAC was negotiated in 1999 and expired in 2003.

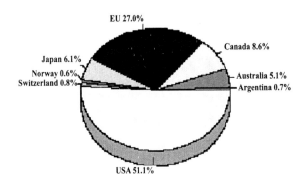

Figure 3. Food Aid Commitments under the Food Aid Convention, 1999.

Under the FAC, the donors could express their annual food aid commitments in either tonnage or in value, but most continue to use the former. Japan is the major exception, although the EU also provides some food aid in the form of cash. The total commitment under the most recent FAC (1999-2003) was 4.9 mmt (see Figure 3 and Appendix Table 2). The United States made the largest commitment, 2.5 mmt or 51% of the total. The combined EU commitment was around 27%. Commitments by Canada, Japan, and Australia were, respectively, 8.6%, 6.1%, and 5.1%. Seven of eight FAC signatories have exceeded their FAC commitments in each of the last six years. Only Argentina has not met its FAC commitment.

Although the FAC expired in 2003, a working committee of the International Grains Council has been established to prepare for its renegotiation.[4] Concurrently, trade-related aspects of food aid are being negotiated in the multilateral trade round known as the Doha Development Agenda (DDA). The Food Aid Committee of the IGC continues to meet periodically to review donor food aid contributions in relation to commitments under the 1999 FAC and to global food needs and has agreed that the existing FAC should be extended for a further two-year period after July 1, 2005. Renegotiation of the FAC, however, appears unlikely until the DDA trade negotiations have been concluded.

Table 1. Annual Commitments under the 1999 Food Aid Convention (metric tons wheat equivalent)

Argentina	35,000	0.72%
Australia	250,000	5.11%
Canada	420,000	8.58%
EU	1,320,000	26.97%
Japan	300,000	6.13%
Norway	30,000	0.61%
Switzerland	40,000	0.82%
USA	2,500,000	51.07%
Total	4,895,000	100.00%

Source: International Grains Council Food Aid Committee, The Food Aid Convention.

ENDNOTES

[1]   Information on the International Grains Council, the Food Aid Convention, and the Food Aid Committee is available at [*http://www.igc.org.uk/*].

[2]   Data on food aid shipments provided by the International Grains Council are reported on a marketing year basis (July-June).

[3]   International Grains Council, Food Aid Committee, *Food Aid Shipments 2002/2003: Report on Shipments by Members of the Food Aid Convention*, July 2004.

[4]   IGC-FAC Press Release, 8 December 2004, available at [*http://www.igc.org.uk/press/ pr041208.htm*].

APPENDIX

Table 1. Food Aid by Major Donor, 1995-2003 (in metric tons wheat equivalent)

	1995/96	1996/97	1997/98	1998/99	1999/00	2000/01	2001/02	2002/03	Total	Annual Average Percent	Annual Average Metric Tons
Argentina	13,400			10,135	2,740				26,275	0.04%	3,284
Australia	298,146	305,127	293,221	273,064	296,713	251,865	245,828	203,820	2,167,784	3.30%	270,973
Canada	448,764	468,431	417,917	487,095	470,640	272,925	393,367	451,537	3,410,676	5.19%	426,335
EU	2,413,991	2,049,691	2,201,162	1,969,892	1,970,768	2,341,277	1,836,717	1,980,781	16,764,279	25.52%	2,095,535
Japan	474,870	326,835	302,626	561,643	337,357	635,158	453,735	668,557	3,760,781	5.73%	470,098
Norway	6,233	32,816	19,306	61,293	75,960	79,857	74,318	134,692	484,475	0.74%	60,559
Switzerland	75,479	38,636	57,915	38,939	61,295	50,804	58,042	67,892	449,002	0.68%	56,125
USA	2,849,384	2,553,283	2,818,500	4,734,121	5,692,116	6,798,280	7,124,407	6,054,197	38,624,288	58.80%	4,828,036
Total	6,580,267	5,774,819	6,110,647	8,136,182	8,907,589	10,430,166	10,186,414	9,561,476	65,687,560	100.00%	8,210,945

Source: International Grains Council Food Aid Committee, *Food Aid Shipments 2001-2003.*

Table 2. Food Aid Contributions to the World Food Program, 1996-2005
(thousand dollars)

	1996	1997	1998	1999	2000	2001	2002	2003	2004	As of April 11, 2005	Total
United States of America	494,980	408,380	876,284	718,856	795,676	1,210,543	933,217	1,459,324	1,044,168	313,021	8,254,449
European Union	603,981	550,522	522,397	461,800	442,495	436,559	560,653	620,929	692,984	295,763	5,188,083
EU Commission	196,873	237,254	184,645	168,098	117,509	118,411	179,205	201,463	200,501	59,059	1,663,017
EU Countries	407,108	313,269	337,752	293,702	324,986	318,149	381,448	419,466	492,483	236,704	3,525,066
Austria	4,774	4,910	3,853	3,710	2,854	1,117	3,302	2,199	2,189	1,165	30,073
Belgium	19,472	17,416	16,908	10,782	6,284	5,294	5,748	8,480	10,750	5,979	107,112
Cyprus*									5		5
Czech Republic*									98	541	639
Denmark	53,064	44,248	43,384	46,900	41,908	39,385	39,964	39,335	43,247	38,887	430,322
Finland	16,045	13,768	13,801	15,345	15,219	14,467	17,445	17,793	17,860	4,071	145,814
France	19,203	21,884	24,742	27,693	26,170	35,929	14,457	14,939	30,288	9,954	225,259
Germany	96,036	68,487	61,779	53,089	46,750	58,088	60,920	46,458	65,126	17,052	573,785
Greece	150	170	25	1	130			200	16	236	928

Table 2. Food Aid Contributions to the World Food Program, 1996–2005 (cont.)
(thousand dollars)

	1996	1997	1998	1999	2000	2001	2002	2003	2004	As of April 11, 2005	Total
Hungary*									65	120	185
Ireland	3,149	4,284	4,378	5,021	7,639	7,317	10,390	11,815	13,684	4,699	72,374
Italy	34,876	9,112	10,632	20,817	19,936	36,060	38,016	40,480	47,613	7,196	264,739
Luxembourg	218		270	130	1,205	1,735	2,919	3,913	5,413	2,746	18,549
Netherlands	78,804	45,972	45,532	55,003	62,801	59,481	58,795	50,422	77,738	62,693	597,241
Poland*									356		356
Slovak. Republic*									25	30	55
Slovenia*									33		33
Spain	13,720	12,245	2,725	2,511	3,256	3,946	2,607	5,357	17,553	3,938	67,858
Sweden	33,164	35,985	29,511	28,415	30,778	27,711	31,167	42,341	44,540	61,879	365,492
United Kingdom	34,434	34,789	80,212	24,284	60,056	27,620	95,718	135,734	115,884	15,518	624,248
Japan	124,032	98,991	123,757	106,438	260,099	91,139	92,896	129,938	135,730	93,781	1,256,801
All Others	222,166	253,647	204,811	268,274	252,853	165,999	222,338	362,983	342,017	176,299	2,471,387
TOTAL	1,445,159	1,311,540	1,727,248	1,555,369	1,751,123	1,904,241	1,809,104	2,573,174	2,214,899	878,864	17,170,720

* Joined European Union in 2004.
Source: World Food Program.

INDEX

Q

R

S

A Solar-Hydrogen Economy

A Solar-Hydrogen Economy
Driving the Green Hydrogen Industrial Revolution

John Mathews

ANTHEM PRESS

Anthem Press
An imprint of Wimbledon Publishing Company
www.anthempress.com

This edition first published in UK and USA 2023
by ANTHEM PRESS
75–76 Blackfriars Road, London SE1 8HA, UK
or PO Box 9779, London SW19 7ZG, UK
and
244 Madison Ave #116, New York, NY 10016, USA

British Library Cataloguing-in-Publication Data
A catalogue record for this book is available from the British Library.

Library of Congress Control Number: 2022942758
A catalog record for this book has been requested.

ISBN-13: 978-1-83998-641-3 (Hbk)
ISBN-10: 1-83998-641-7 (Hbk)
ISBN-13: 978-1-83998-642-0 (Pbk)
ISBN-10: 1-83998-642-5 (Pbk)

This title is also available as an e-book.

CONTENTS

ABSTRACT

In this study, I depict a green hydrogen economy as a potential successor to and replacement of the fossil fuel economy in its entirety. To think like this promotes a sense of the vast scale required to resolve the problems created by fossil fuel dependence. I characterize this view as a total substitution perspective. By contrast, mainstream depictions of the green shift have typically focused on changes at the margin – substitution of renewables in place of coal-fired power generation, or battery storage as a means of evening out flows of green energy; while economists have offered carbon taxes or cap and trade schemes as 'solutions' to the global warming crisis. I argue that these are simply comparative static interventions that do not engage with the real industrial dynamics of the transition. In this study instead I go well beyond the introduction of renewables to encompass the comprehensive role to be played by green hydrogen not just in power generation but across heavy industry (steel, cement, glass and fertilizers) and in heavy, long-haul transport (battery and fuel-cell electric vehicles, trucks, trains, ships and aircraft). I depict the resulting transition to green hydrogen as encompassing the entire industrial system that is currently dependent on fossil fuels – all 12 billion tonnes of oil-equivalent per year, calling for its energy-equivalent replacement by the production of 4 billion tonnes of green hydrogen per year. We are witnessing the rise of a new giant in the world of energy. Accordingly, in place of simple comparative static economic reasoning, I deploy concepts from heterodox economics (increasing returns, circular and cumulative causation, creative destruction and chain reactions within and between clusters) to present a synoptic view of the hydrogen-propelled green transition as a systemic – dynamic and interactive – process. Since this transition will involve *manufacturing* our energy in place of drilling, mining or otherwise extracting fuels created by nature, this process has the potential to be the greatest social and economic transformation of our time. The barriers standing in the way are many, and call for superior political, economic and business strategies to overcome them. Ultimately, the green industrial transition has to succeed, as it offers the only genuine solution to the existential crisis facing our industrial civilization traced to our wanton burning of fossil fuels.

ANALYTICAL CONTENTS

ACRONYMS

AEM	Anionic Exchange Membrane (electrolysis)
AREH	Asian Renewable Energy Hub (Western Australia)
AWE	Alkaline Water Electrolysis
BESS	Battery Energy Storage System
BEV	Battery Electric Vehicle
CBI	Climate Bonds Initiative
CCC	Circular & Cumulative Causation
CCS	Carbon Capture & Storage
CFE	Capillary-Fed Electrolysis
CSP	Concentrated Solar Power
DAE	Direct Air Electrolysis
DRI	Direct Reduced Iron
EAF	Electric Arc Furnace
FCEV	Fuel-Cell Electric Vehicle
FFs	Fossil Fuels
FFI	Fortescue Future Industries (Aus)
GEM	Green Energy Manufacturing centre/hub (e.g. based at Gladstone (Qld))
GGE	Green Growth Economy
GH$_2$	Green Hydrogen
HB	Haber-Bosch process (ammonia)
HESC	Hydrogen Energy Supply Chain (Japan-Australia consortium)
HPU	Hydrogen Producing Unit (module)
HRS	Hydrogen Refuelling Station
HSC	Hydrogen Supply Chain
HYBRIT	Hydrogen Breakthrough Iron-making Technology (Sweden)
ICE	Internal Combustion Engine
INDCs	Intended Nationally Determined Contributions (Paris Agreement)
IPCC	Intergovernmental Panel on Climate Change (UN)
IRENA	International Renewable Energy Agency
LCRs	Local Content Requirements
LOHC	Liquid Organic Hydrogen Carrier (e.g. methanol)
NGO	Non-Governmental Organization
OER	Oxygen Evolution Reaction (water electrolysis)
P2F	Power to Fuel
PAE	Pressurized Alkaline Electrolysis

PEM	Polymer Electrolyte Membrane cell
PEME	Proton Exchange Membrane Electrolysis
PEMFC	Proton Exchange Membrane Fuel Cell
PVC	Photovoltaic Cell
RIL	Reliance Industries Ltd (India)
S-HES	Solar-Hydrogen Energy System (Bockris)
SHE	Solar-Hydrogen Economy
SMR	Steam Methane Reforming
SOE	Solid Oxide Electrolysis
TEP	Techno-Economic Paradigm
UNFCCC	UN Framework Convention on Climate Change
WTO	World Trade Organization

ACKNOWLEDGEMENTS

I would like to acknowledge the thoughtful and helpful comments of Professors Jan Fagerberg, Rainer Kattel, Keun Lee, Carlota Perez, Gerhard Swiegers, Nick Vonortas and Linda Weiss, and of Drs Arkebe Oqubay and Michael Peck on earlier drafts of this text, as well as the contribution to the charts from Ms Carol X. Huang. Long-standing discussions on the energy transition in East Asia with my colleagues Dr Elizabeth Thurbon, Dr Sung-Young Kim and Dr Hao Tan are gratefully acknowledged. The usual disclaimers apply.

Chapter 1

INTRODUCTION

A half-century ago, the South African electrochemist John O'Malley Bockris invented the modern world. He formulated the concept of the 'hydrogen economy' as a sustainable industrial system that could replace all fossil fuels in an industrial economy in their entirety. His motivation was to prevent anticipated runaway global warming and to reduce dependence on finite fossil fuel reserves – two issues that were then just emerging and which have only become more pressing in the intervening years. He called this system a 'solar-hydrogen energy system' where hydrogen is the core feature: it would be produced via electrolysis of water, utilizing solar power (encompassing wind power) as a source of renewable power and channelling the green hydrogen as input into numerous industrial pathways to replace carbon-based inputs – for example hydrogen steel, hydrogen cement, hydrogen aluminium and various hydrogen chemicals, particularly green ammonia as the basis of the global fertilizer industry and hydrogen fuel cells for heavy transport (trains, buses, ships and aircraft). The 'burning' of hydrogen in all these pathways would produce nothing but water – thus creating a grand cycle which starts with water and powers an entire industrial economy to produce water as the final product once again, round and round in an endless circular hydrogen economy.[1]

This ingenious conception, which had been intimated by the British scientist J. B. S. Haldane a half-century earlier (in 1923 in a lecture at Cambridge), is now finally coming to fruition as the world races to find a solution to climate change.[2] Humanity is in a desperate struggle to create a post-fossil fuels economy as the only known means of avoiding terminal climate change induced by our profligate burning of fossil fuels in the twentieth century. In the intervening half-century, since Bockris' work appeared in the 1970s, we

---

1 See the early intimations of the solar-hydrogen energy system in Bockris' letter to *Science* (1972) and his book-length treatment in 1975, *Energy: The Solar-Hydrogen Alternative*, and further elaboration in Bockris (2013) and Bockris and Veziroglu (1985).
2 See Haldane's article based on his lecture: Haldane (1923).

have witnessed the concept of the solar-hydrogen economy hijacked by the fossil fuels industry – pushing for 'brown hydrogen' sourced from coal or 'grey hydrogen' sourced from natural gas without carbon capture and storage (CCS) or 'blue hydrogen' sourced from natural gas with CCS, and by the nuclear industry pushing for 'pink hydrogen' sourced from nuclear-powered electrolysis of water. These colour-coded options are all backward-looking alternatives, designed to extend the life of fossil and nuclear fuels, as compared with the future-focused direct solar-powered version of the hydrogen economy, which is fundamentally green, safe and sustainable.

Now – almost at a minute to midnight – there is a serious green hydrogen industrial revolution underway. Governments and international agencies are bidding to take the lead in scaling up their efforts, while industrialists like Andrew 'Twiggy' Forrest in Australia or Mukesh Ambani in India and their companies are retrieving the original conception of the solar-hydrogen economy as formulated originally by Bockris and bypassing fossil fuel and nuclear claims on our future. This emergent industrial revolution is tapping enormous renewable (solar and wind) resources for electrolysis of water at vast scale to power a comprehensive, global green hydrogen industrial economy – one that is relatively pollution free and devoid of carbon emissions and one that can replace fossil fuels *in their entirety*. The revolution is as yet in its infancy. But there are unmistakeable signs that it is underway and propelled by drivers that promise far-reaching outcomes. It is time to take the solar-hydrogen economy seriously and plan for its imminent arrival.

As Forrest himself says: 'There will be no bigger industry' in the future than green hydrogen and ammonia. 'It will dwarf the scale of iron ore, it will dwarf the scale of coal'.[3] Forrest estimates the size of a green hydrogen industry to be $12 trillion by 2050 – making it by far the largest industry on the planet. These are prescient remarks from an industrialist who has looked deeply at the emergent green hydrogen industry and plans to swing his company behind this fundamental new trend, creating a specialized vehicle for this project in *Fortescue Future Industries.*

The idea of a solar-hydrogen economy extends well beyond its precursors in the form of renewable energies and circular commodity flows. Yes, renewables are needed as the source of energy, in the form of the green hydrogen produced through electrolysis of water. But then the green hydrogen can be stored or flow through the economy along multiple pathways to produce green steel, or green cement for construction, or green ammonia-based fertilizers

---

3 See: Don't deny green energy future: Forrest | Dixon Financial Group (dixonfg. com.au).

for agriculture. In this way, the conception of the solar-hydrogen economy extends well beyond that of the renewables themselves, and insofar as the hydrogen originates from water and returns to water as it is 'burnt', it encapsulates the essence of the circular economy.[4] My object in this book is to give the reader the sense that a green hydrogen transition is already underway and at a scale that it could conceivably substitute for fossil fuels – provided the numerous obstacles being placed in its path can be circumvented.

To gain a feel for the needed scale of this hydrogen-based industrial system, it suffices to think in terms of a molecule of hydrogen replacing a molecule of hydrocarbon or a molecule of water replacing a molecule of carbon dioxide in almost every industrial process requiring heat.[5] So the scale of the solar-hydrogen economy is necessarily vast. Huge arrays of solar cells and wind turbines that are part of the energy transition will serve to produce the green hydrogen that will then oust the existing fossil fuels as the hydrogen flows through the industrial economy. As the scale of the solar-hydrogen economy grows, so the reach of fossil fuels will decline – until (by perhaps 2050) the fossils will have dwindled to no more than small uses as petrochemical inputs or lubricants and no longer serve primarily as fuel. Almost all fuel requirements would by then be met by green hydrogen.

So a solar-hydrogen economy can be characterized as consisting of an energy component (largely renewable) and a material flow component (largely circular) encompassing the entire industrial economy. The energy component features renewable energies at a vast, terawatt scale, being used to generate electric power for immediate use (e.g. as fuel cell vehicles or domestic power consumption) or green hydrogen via electrolysis or some comparable system like photocatalysis for further industrial transformation. The material flow component of the solar-hydrogen economy consists of a circular flow of green hydrogen (starting with water and ending with water) together with the materials used to create and sustain the hydrogen flows. Hydrogen is the primary energy vector together with derivatives like ammonia (a compound of nitrogen and hydrogen with the formula NH_3) or methanol (methyl alcohol),

---

4 Of course, this macro-view conceals all manner of smaller complications like water-containing electrolytes which present technical but not insuperable issues. For a breakthrough that exploits water-containing electrolytes, pursued at the Argonne National Laboratory of the US Department of Energy, see 'Water-containing electrolyte might transform battery production', *Engineering & Technology*, 3 May 2022, at: Water-containing electrolyte might transform battery production | E&T Magazine (theiet.org).

5 On the technical aspects of the various processes through which hydrogen can flow, both as reactant and source of heat, see for example Lebrouhi et al (2022) or the Goldman Sachs 2022 report *The rise of clean hydrogen*.

which can be used as energy store or fuel (e.g. in ships powered by fuel cells or aircraft likewise powered by fuel cells or burning green hydrogen as thermal fuel). Most significantly hydrogen will be used to generate heat in heavy process industries like steel, cement, aluminium or glass or fertilizer production and for their subsequent use in heavy engineering (e.g. roads, bridges, shipbuilding and automotive) and agriculture. These various pathways for the transformation of green hydrogen and its derivatives provide new value chains that generate direct substitution for extant fossil fuels. The ultimate test of this emergent solar-hydrogen energy system (SHES) as an alternative energy economy is this: does it generate opportunities (in principle) to replace fossil fuels in their entirety? Anything less is just fiddling at the margin.

Of course, the transformation will not be overnight: it will take decades to complete. No genuine industrial revolution can be accomplished without involving multiple industrial pathways and technological choices taking time to mature. But the beauty of the schema is that for every pathway involving green hydrogen displacing fossil fuels, the solar-hydrogen economy comes one step closer, and the system based on fossil fuels correspondingly declines, thus bringing more momentum behind the transition. The process reinforces itself through positive feedback in what maverick economists describe as an economic chain reaction (e.g. Kaldor 1970) or as circular and cumulative causation. This latter concept, associated with the great development economist Gunnar Myrdal, has fallen into disuse in mainstream economics. But its relevance to the green transition is clear and immediate and generates insights not otherwise available.[6]

John O'Malley Bockris formulated his brilliant conception of the SHES (noting that he never used this acronym himself) while working in an Australian university, at the School of Physical Sciences at Flinders University in Adelaide. He published the ideas in a letter to *Science* in 1972 and at book length in 1975 – but he never lived to see the idea being taken up in earnest as it is today. It was visionaries like Bockris and Haldane who first saw in detail the miracle of hydrogen as a sustainable alternative and successor to fossil fuels in their entirety. What an extraordinary development that we as a civilization should have powered our way to wealth through the discovery of fossil fuels, and then having reached our present state of wealth but coming up against the impasse of global warming, that we should find a benign

---

6 See Kaldor (1970) for an exposition of the notion of economic chain reaction or Myrdal (1957) for a discussion of circular and cumulative causation. Both Myrdal and Kaldor worked on the concepts together when they were with the UN Economic Commission for Europe.

alternative that can act as successor to the fossil fuels economy. No one could have predicted this astonishing sequence of developments in advance of their recent appearance. To a time-travelling observer from the eighteenth century, it would be quite incredible. Yet it falls to us in the twenty-first century to bring this sequence to fruition.

An All-Encompassing Industrial Revolution

Bockris' vision was all-encompassing, spanning substitution by green hydrogen in all aspects of the fossil fuels economy. It included not just transport applications (fuel cell electric vehicles, heavy trucks, trains, ships and aircraft) and domestic applications but even more significantly the substitution of fossil fuels by hydrogen in heavy process industries.[7] In this text, I update his technical formulations and put the solar-hydrogen economy in a broader international political economy perspective that focuses on the drivers as well as obstacles to its eventual arrival. Whereas Bockris displayed a somewhat naïve optimism in his formulations, our task now is to confront the difficulties and find ways to overcome them – as I do in this book.

It is the breadth of vision and scale of application that is the signature of the emergent solar-hydrogen economy. Thus at the very dawn of the hydrogen economy, Bockris was here putting his finger on the key issue that would drive green hydrogen as a successor to the fossil fuel economy – not so much the issue of electrified transport but the substitution of carbon by hydrogen in heavy engineering and industry. As each substitution is accomplished, the world moves closer to a 100 per cent solar-hydrogen economy – one where green hydrogen supply chains start with water to produce green hydrogen (GH_2), and trace it through the principal value-adding chains involving industrial heat production in industries such as steel, cement, aluminium, glass, fertilizers (ammonia) and chemicals, in which processes the green hydrogen is 'burnt' to produce water. It is the flow of green hydrogen through the industrial economy both as a reactant itself and in its various chemical derivative forms which makes up the core of the emergent green hydrogen economy.

---

7 As Bockris said in his 1972 letter to *Science*: 'Iron ore could be economically reduced by hydrogen directly to iron, the airborne excess product being steam. At plasma temperatures aluminium could be produced more cheaply by thermal reduction of aluminium oxide by hydrogen than by present methods ... Ammonia could be produced at about half the present price' (Bockris 1972: 1323). Note how these are strikingly accurate forecasts of where hydrogen might be profitably used in process industries like steel, glass or aluminium. See A Hydrogen Economy (science.org).

This is a grand cycle indeed, from water to water – the ultimate in clean renewability and recyclability. The alternative colour-coded forms of hydrogen derived from fossil fuels do not share in this grand planetary water cycle conception of a future industrial economy. Water is abundant, in most parts of the world. But even where it is in short supply, there is an abundant source of water from the air (Aqua Aeram) or from the sea (involving desalination e.g. Sundrop farms) – both now being developed as active alternatives to fossil fuel options.[8]

The hydrogen economy has been a goal for at least the last half-century, but it has been hijacked too many times by the fossil fuels and nuclear power sectors, bringing the concept into disrepute. But now climate change has acted as the spur to drive adoption of green hydrogen along multiple pathways, and at vastly increasing scale, so that a real green hydrogen revolution is unfolding – in such a way that fossil fuels could be well on the way to obsolescence by 2030 or 2040 and be almost extinct (apart from their use as petrochemical inputs) by mid-century.

And let us be clear that there is no other way to curb climate change. The green hydrogen industrial revolution is the essential process needed to decarbonize and transform heavy industry from a polluting curse to a clean and green industrial future. At what scale does this need to happen? At a vast scale – at the scale that replaces fossil fuels in their entirety by hydrogen sourced from renewables. We are talking about *an industrial system that is an alternative and successor to the fossil fuels system in its entirety*. It will call for the generation of terawatts of green power and its sourcing of billions of tonnes of green hydrogen each year via electrolysis to produce more than enough hydrogen to take over completely from coal, natural gas and oil.[9]

What is potentially being created is nothing less than a vast new set of industries that will provide clean energy, power, clean fuel for transport and above all clean inputs to heavy engineering and industry, all at a scale that will eventually make fossil fuels (in principle) redundant. Of course, it won't happen overnight: the industrial investments involved will take decades to accomplish. And fossil fuels will never go extinct – their complex molecules will always be of great relevance as petrochemical inputs on account of their beautiful molecular architecture. What a waste to just burn them and

---

8 Work on Direct Air Electrolysis (DAE) was reported in 2022 by Guo et al (2022). See the industrial proposal for large-scale electrolysis of water from the air, by Aqua Aeram, at *Desert Bloom Hydrogen*: Desert Bloom Hydrogen | Aqua Aerem (aqua-aerem. com). On the Sundrop Farms project for enhanced agriculture, see Sundrop Farms - A fresh way of growing - Redefining sustainable greenhouse.

9 International energy agencies have started to address the challenges of transitioning to a green hydrogen economy. See for example IEA (2019) or IRENA (2020).

extract their heat energy – the least interesting aspect of these remarkable commodities.

The goal of this short book is to outline what kind of industrial revolution is needed to create a global solar-hydrogen energy economy – just as envisaged by John O'Malley Bockris – but updated to the 2020s. What is the evidence that initial steps are already being taken? The scale of solar and wind arrays needed to produce the terawatts of renewable power is now known and understood. Arrays of tens and even hundreds of gigawatts scale are now being built – in Australia or North Africa or South America, for example.[10] And the gigawatts of electrolyzer capacity needed to produce the billions of tonnes of green hydrogen are also known and understood. There remains the challenge of actually building these arrays and electrolyzer stacks. There remains the challenge of overcoming the obstacles to this systemic change. These are challenges that can surely be met, through the politics of the clean energy transition. Bold political leadership is called for.

It is striking that in early 2022 there has been not a single political leader in the West who has grasped the full significance of the solar-hydrogen alternative and fashioned a political programme around its achievement.[11] Here is surely an opportunity for an imaginative leader to step forward.

Our appreciation of the simplicity and beauty of the green hydrogen industrial vision is quite recent. In my 2015 book *Greening of Capitalism*, I did not discuss green hydrogen at all. Indeed, there was not even a mention of hydrogen in the Index. The debunking text *The Hype about Hydrogen*, by Joseph Romm, had come out in 2004, and had cast a pall of suspicion over all plans to do with hydrogen – on the grounds that almost all of them in the decade leading to that book's appearance had involved some extension of the life of fossil fuels, and was invariably accompanied by a lot of hot air – the hype about hydrogen. My 2015 book failed to appreciate the shift that was already occurring, in putting *green hydrogen* derived from electrolysis of water using renewables power, at the centre of analysis. This mistake is not to be repeated.

---

10 Investments in large-scale arrays of wind turbines and solar arrays are now routinely reported. For a recent overview, see my article on the Sun Cable project in northern Australia, with colleagues Elizabeth Thurbon, Sung-Young Kim and Hao Tan, in *The Conversation* (26 February 2020) at: It might sound 'batshit insane' but Australia could soon export sunshine to Asia via a 3,800km cable (theconversation.com).

11 Ironically it was US president George W. Bush who came closest, in his speech of 6 February 2003, when he called for a hydrogen economy – albeit with all the fossil fuel trimmings. See: The Hydrogen Fuel Cell Scam — From George W. Bush & 'The Big 3' To Toyota, Honda, & Japan – by David Mazovick, *CleanTechnica*, 2 January 2019.

Now it is not just the fossil fuel companies that are promoting hydrogen (in their own way), but a raft of other companies that are emerging as green champions, and that have nothing to do with fossil fuels. Now it is giant investment banks like Goldman Sachs or PwC that are driving debate over the emergent green hydrogen economy, taking a clear-eyed perspective on the quite different trajectory of green hydrogen from its grey, blue or pink hydrogen competitors with their links to fossil fuels or to nuclear power.[12] (If anyone needed a reason to oppose the 'left' environmental case for nuclear power, as formulated by e.g. The Breakthrough Institute, it is that the solar-hydrogen alternative promises endless supplies and zero marginal costs for hydrogen as the principal energy vector of a post-fossil fuels industrial civilization, while 'pink' nuclear-powered electrolysis of water offers no advantages over solar and copious disadvantages.[13])

Financing the Solar-Hydrogen Transition

The solar-hydrogen energy revolution promises to involve trillions of watts in renewable power and in electrolyzer stacks, calling for investments in the trillions of dollars. Where are these funds to come from? Part of the weakness of the UN approach to mitigation of climate change is that financing has always been viewed as being provided from public (i.e. tax-based) sources. This is a dead-end solution, almost guaranteed to fail. Yet it is obvious that the great capital markets of capitalism, for debt ($100 trillion bonds market) and equity ($50 trillion stock markets), must be mobilized. And they are being mobilized! In 2021 green bonds worth $0.5 trillion were issued, with the NGO Climate Bonds Initiative forecasting $1 trillion in green bonds issuance in 2022 and $5 trillion by 2025. This is what we might call 'serious finance'.[14]

---

12 Of the major investment banks, Goldman Sachs is the lead promoter of the green hydrogen revolution, issuing a major report in July 2020 following up with a further report in February 2022 on the clean hydrogen revolution; see *The Clean Hydrogen Revolution* (February 2022) at: Portrait (goldmansachs.com). PwC is issuing bold analyses of the trends towards a green hydrogen economy; see *The Green Hydrogen Economy: Predicting the decarbonisation agenda of tomorrow*, at: Green hydrogen economy - predicted development of tomorrow: PwC.

13 For a typical example of this misguided reasoning, see The Breakthrough Institute, 2014, *The Nuclear Power Imperative*, at: The Nuclear Power Imperative | The Breakthrough Institute.

14 See successive reports by CBI culminating in the most recent 2021 report: $500bn Green Issuance 2021: social and sustainable acceleration: Annual green $1tn in sight: Market expansion forecasts for 2022 and 2025 | Climate Bonds Initiative.

Let's be clear as to how the debt capital markets (bond markets) work. Let's say a bank or other financial institution becomes involved in raising finance for a green project (say, building an array of green hydrogen electrolyzers) and does so by issuing a green bond. That bond is simply a piece of paper (virtual paper) that promises the bearer a specified return each year, based on the earnings of the green project being financed. So the electrolyzer project will have to be well managed, and the forecast earnings will have to materialize. If not, then the reaction of the bond market is likely to be savage, and the bank's standing is likely to be severely downgraded. If it is a country issuing the green bond as an aspect of its sovereign debt, then the country has to be scrupulous in its management of the green project – because if it is careless, or allows the management of the project to pass from responsible to irresponsible hands, then the bond market can downgrade the country's sovereign wealth standing – with the threat that national bankruptcy may result.

So bonds are not to be played with. But if used carefully and sensibly, they provide a powerful tool in redirecting capital investment away from fossil fuels projects to green projects, of which green hydrogen projects promise to be at the forefront in coming years. Once finance swings behind the utilization of the bond markets (twice as large globally as the equity (stock) markets), it has virtually unlimited funds to draw from, as investors shift away from fossil fuels projects with all their risks and uncertainties and look for safer and more sustainable green investments.

Green hydrogen offers a unique possibility then of scaling up a green industrial revolution that can replace in its entirety the extant fossil fuel system, while green bonds offer a (near) limitless source of investment funds (up to $100 trillion) that work with the dynamics of capitalism and not against them. We are witnessing the emergence of a new giant of the world of energy. Just how this unique combination of developments has come to pass, and how its emergence transforms the politics of energy and climate change, remains to be elucidated in the pages that follow.

Chapter 2

A SOLAR-HYDROGEN ECONOMY

Energy is the lifeblood of the industrial economy. For many centuries, humanity laboured to transform materials and grow food using only animal and human muscle power, with some exceptions using wind and water power (wind and water mills to grind grains, ships fitted with sails propelled by wind) and of course burning wood or charcoal for domestic and small-scale industrial heat. Then along came the industrial revolution and the supreme innovation of fossil fuels – initially coal, then oil and then gas. Fossil fuels were a miracle that allowed our industrial civilization to break through age-old Malthusian constraints. Fossil fuels were put to use at scale by Western countries such as those in Europe and the United States. As their energy consumption grew so too did their wealth. An enormous gap in wealth and income opened up between the West and 'the Rest' – notably China and India, two ancient civilizations that missed out on the fossil fuelled industrial revolution. In the twentieth century, countries in East Asia led by Japan worked out how to close the gap with the West by state-led technology leverage strategies.[1] Now in the twenty-first century, China and India are claiming their place in the sun and are learning the lessons of state-led industrialization from Japan, Korea and Taiwan. But they are being forced to do so at a scale far larger than the original industrializers – and this is having severe repercussions as the scale of fossil fuel usage multiplies.

As fossil fuel usage expands, everyone agrees that climate change is the overwhelming issue to be dealt with in the twenty-first century, and finding a path towards a post-fossil fuels future is the only solution we have. Climate change is the existential threat faced by our industrial civilization. And yet the economics of the transition are almost invariably discussed in the simplest and most elementary forms. It seems that commentators feel that the 'need' for a post-fossil fuels energy system is sufficient to call such a system into

---

1 See my study of the rise of the semiconductor industry in East Asia, conducted jointly with Cho Dong-Sung of the Seoul National University (Mathews and Cho 2000).

existence. All you need is a price on carbon – and, hey presto, the world of fossil fuels magically fades away.

If only things were that simple. So many commentaries on climate change and global warming make the point that industry, transport and domestic heating all need to be decarbonized – but rarely venture further to discuss just how this process is to be accomplished in any detail. In this text, I tackle this question by positing the green industrial revolution that is really needed, which will involve a vast expansion of renewable energy generation and the search for a substitute for carbon in domestic and industrial heating and heavy transport processes. We are fortunate in finding a strong and feasible substitute in the form of hydrogen – an element which can be generated from water (using electrolysis powered by renewables) and which as it is utilized in industry or transport (as it is 'burnt') simply generates water again – in a vast cycle that starts and ends with water. Nothing could be cleaner in providing a foundation for industry that has no link to carbon and has zero carbon emissions.

I suggest that the best name for this alternative energy-industrial system is the *solar-hydrogen economy*, meaning that hydrogen is the principal energy store and carrier and that it is derived ultimately from solar energy (usually via solar-powered electrolysis of water). Such a name makes it abundantly clear that the energy system that drives industry need have no further reliance on fossil fuels and their carbon footprint. The promise of hydrogen produced from solar power (encompassing wind power as well) is that it can replace fossil fuels *in their entirety* – lock, stock and barrel.[2] The issue is: can this replacement be accomplished at a sufficient scale and in a sufficiently short time to fend off global warming and its numerous deleterious consequences.

A solar-hydrogen economy based on green hydrogen sourced from the electrolysis of water is to be distinguished from other sources that do not share the circular flow characteristics of green hydrogen. As noted above, brown hydrogen comes from coal; grey hydrogen comes from natural gas without carbon capture and storage (CCS); blue hydrogen comes from natural gas with CCS (although very few examples are practised). None of these options dispenses with fossil fuels nor engages with a global water cycle in the manner of green hydrogen. Pink hydrogen sourced from water via electrolysis using nuclear power is simply a high-cost and high-risk version of green hydrogen – and who would wish for that if the lower cost (and diminishing cost) version, sourced from the sun, is clearly available.

---

2 Solar power can encompass wind power as well because it is ultimately solar input that moves the air in ways that we experience as wind.

A solar-hydrogen economy thus provides a broad descriptive term for a successor to the fossil fuels energy system, without necessarily specifying the technologies of hydrogen production nor the pathways through the economy traced out by green hydrogen. In this sense, the term promises to provide a broad goal for the green industrial revolution as well as a descriptor that is unlikely to change fundamentally in future years. We are discussing 'a' solar-hydrogen economy, where the indefinite article leaves open numerous opportunities for reaching the post-fossil fuels goal, whereas the definite article would tend to close off options. Better to see the future as open-ended.

Any version of a solar-hydrogen economy would be based fundamentally on manufacturing, in the sense that all devices needed – electrolyzers, renewables devices, batteries and fuel cells, fuel cell electric vehicles (FCEVs), pipelines, recharging stations and much else – are products of manufacturing. We can view this as a maturing of the energy system, which would no longer have to depend on fossil fuels with their haphazard energy allocations in the earth's crust; we could instead take charge of the production of energy through manufactured systems, that is systems produced by ourselves. No longer would energy be 'free' in the sense that it is a free gift of nature, granted to some to be able to extract fuels from the earth and denied to others – with all the deleterious geopolitical consequences of this.[3] With hydrogen, we must work hard for our energy, by manufacturing the devices that can transform solar energy income into usable energy systems and distribute this energy (in the form of hydrogen or ammonia) along multiple industrial pathways. There are renewable devices themselves – solar PV cells and wind turbines. And then there are the devices that make the solar-hydrogen economy run – the electrolyzers, the fuel cells, the hydrogen refuelling systems, all of them products of manufacturing. Energy would no longer be 'free' to be dug or drilled from the earth. With hydrogen, our industrial civilization would finally come of age with an energy strategy that is knowingly based on our capacity to manufacture our way to wealth.[4]

---

3 Of course, solar power generation also depends on manufacture of solar PV cells with their material requirements – but it can be anticipated that these materials would increasingly be supplied by circular flows (recycling and 'urban mining'). For a survey of the issues involved, as well as examples of recent practice, see the IRENA report *End of Life Management: Solar Photovoltaic Panels*, IRENA, 2016, at: End-of-life management: Solar Photovoltaic Panels (irena.org).

4 At the time of writing, the unprovoked Russian invasion of Ukraine is in full swing, where Putin's Russia earns precious foreign reserves through its sale of oil, gas and coal to the European Union. Debate on curbing Russia's ability to finance its invasion is focused on financial sanctions and potentially on capping the price to be paid

The solar-hydrogen conception is as simple as it is transcending. All energy in this conception is sourced ultimately from the sun.[5] Energy pathways start with the generation of solar power, through photovoltaic cells or some other process like concentrated solar power. At a scale of terawatts (now being approached in sun-drenched places like Australia or North Africa, where gigawatt-scale solar arrays are becoming common) this generates abundant clean power, which can be utilized as electricity to power electric motors or converted to clean energy storage as green hydrogen via electrolysis. The green hydrogen can then be stored and drive multiple conversion pathways, just like oil today – as transport fuel, as input into heavy process industries like steel, cement or fertilizers, as chemicals feedstock and as heating vector. As hydrogen is utilized – 'burnt' – so it produces water as the only 'waste' product. It's an industrial system that starts with water and ends with water – in a grand cycle that can be repeated over and over again in perpetuity.

A green hydrogen economy goes beyond previous discussions of a renewable energy revolution in that the hydrogen is sourced from renewables but in addition it is envisaged at such scale that it can provide fuel for transport and heavy industrial processes as well as material inputs that can substitute for fossil fuels in their entirety. As such, a solar-hydrogen economy is a conceptual leap forward beyond the introduction of renewables into the world's power systems; it depends on renewables to produce the green hydrogen in the first place, but it is envisaged as providing the fuels and material flows that have previously been dominated (both conceptually and materially) by fossil fuels. Now it is the entire fossil fuels energy system that is at stake. It is the industrial revolution to end all industrial revolutions. We can count ourselves extremely fortunate as an industrial civilization to have stumbled on such a profoundly favourable successor to the fossil fuels system.

Characteristics of a Solar-Hydrogen Economy

Let us tease out the characteristics of a solar-hydrogen cycle and the economy that it generates. It is clean (no carbon), sustainable (renewable), safe (no

---

for these fossil fuel exports. A solar hydrogen economy would be immune to such developments. See 'How to stop Russia immediately' by German Galushchenko and Oleg Ustenko, *Project Syndicate*, 23 June 2022, at: How to Stop Russia Immediately by German Galushchenko & Oleg Ustenko - Project Syndicate (project-syndicate.org).

5 Energy is sourced directly from the sun (solar power) or indirectly, as in wind power. Higher latitudes that receive less sunlight can store the energy received (via batteries or hydro-storage or as hydrogen) or can trade energy products with countries that receive an abundance of sunlight.

nasties) and democratic (available to all). The only problematic issue is this: can it be scaled up in time to save the planet? Let us tackle these questions one by one (in reverse order).

Scale of the hydrogen economy: 4 billion tonnes per year

I am depicting a solar-hydrogen economy as a substitute for fossil fuels in their entirety. How large then would the solar-hydrogen system have to be? The extant fossil fuels economy – based on oil, coal and gas – has grown to vast dimensions over the past century and more. According to the International Energy Agency (IEA), fossil fuel production in 2021 was close to 12 billion tonnes of oil equivalent, providing a vast energy flow of just under 500 exajoule (EJ) per year.[6] To give a feel for the scale involved, energy at the level of 1 EJ is found in volcanic eruptions and earthquakes. For example, the 2011 Tohoku earthquake followed by tsunami in Japan registered an energy level of 1.4 EJ. So 500 EJ is 360 times that energy level – truly a colossal level of energy mobilized by the fossil fuels industry. Looking at the different fossil fuels, oil itself is produced at a scale of close to 100 million barrels per day, or around 4.5 billion tonnes of oil per year. In energy terms, this is 190 EJ (or 190×10^{18} joules) in a year. Natural gas is produced at a scale of 140 EJ, and coal at a scale of 160 EJ, making fossil fuels in their entirety work at an energy level of just under 500 EJ in a year – a truly vast amount of energy.[7]

So how much green hydrogen would be needed to substitute for the entire incumbent oil, coal and gas energy system? Taking the energy content of hydrogen as being between a lower level of 120 MJ per kg (or 120 GJ per tonne) and an upper level of 142 GJ per tonne (say, 125 GJ per tonne) this would call for 4 Gt of hydrogen (4 billion tonnes) per year. By comparison, the world currently uses 4.5 billion tonnes of oil per year. So more or less the same tonnage of hydrogen as oil used today would substitute in energy terms not just for the oil but for all the coal and gas used as well. This gives a sense of what a powerful energy source hydrogen really is. It also gives a sense of the scale of the hydrogen economy needed to substitute entirely for fossil fuels.

---

6 Fossil fuels production in 2021 was 11.7 Gtoe billion tonnes oil equivalent, or in energy terms, 490 EJ; see IEA *World Energy Balances*, at: World – World Energy Balances: Overview – Analysis – IEA.

7 These data are based on the annual *BP Statistical Review of Global Energy* (2021 edition): Statistical Review of World Energy | Energy economics | Home (bp.com) as well as the International Energy Agency, *World Energy Balances*, at: World – World Energy Balances: Overview – Analysis – IEA.

The 4 billion tonnes of green hydrogen needed to substitute for all fossil fuels each year is not to be sourced from mineral deposits, as is the case with fossil fuels. Instead, the needed hydrogen is to be produced by manufacturing – utilizing manufactured products like electrolyzers to split water for the production of hydrogen, and solar PV cells and wind turbines for generation of the green power needed to run the electrolyzers. This is the fundamental point of distinction separating the solar-hydrogen era from the extant fossil fuels era.

Manufacturing available to all

So a solar-hydrogen energy-industrial system is one based on manufacturing, not mining or extraction of energy resources from the earth. While industry was tied to fossil fuels, there was always an element of randomness as to which country or region had access to fossil fuels. The former prime minister of Israel, Golda Meir, used to joke that if God favoured Israel (as Jews claimed) then why did he give the Arabs all the oil? The joke wouldn't work in a solar-hydrogen economy, because in such an economy energy security is ensured through building manufacturing industries. To build a solar-hydrogen system, one utilizes factors under our own control – one needs solar power converters (manufactured as e.g. photovoltaic cells) and electrolyzers to split water – all products of manufacturing. And the manufacturing itself can be made more and more circular, recycling materials ('urban mining') rather than digging them from the earth.[8] So a solar-hydrogen system is one based on manufacturing which is increasingly circular, and so under human control – rather than subject to the arbitrary and haphazard allocations of fuels and commodities to countries and regions resulting in their randomly allocated geopolitical dependence on the fossil fuelled system.[9]

Manufacturing is essentially democratic in that it is a means to wealth generation which is (potentially) available to all. Any country or government can embark on the manufacturing projects needed to power a solar-hydrogen economy. It does not have to dance to the tune of the oil companies and their

---

8 Of course, the green transition will involve reliance on new minerals like lithium and cobalt for batteries and rare earths for renewables devices and electrolyzer catalysts. I do not seek to minimize these issues in advancing the concept of an expanding circular flow economy. But they are not insuperable problems.

9 In the words of Oliver Yates, then head of Australia's Clean Energy Finance Corporation, 'We like the hydrogen space, it is versatile, transportable and flexible … and it is economic in regional Australia right now'. See Garnaut, CEFC push hydrogen to make Australia renewable power-house | *RenewEconomy*.

deadly games – although the most far-sighted of them will certainly play a positive role in its achievement. The difference is that manufacturing can be performed anywhere, by anyone – as contrasted with oil drilling or coal mining, which can only be done where the resources are haphazardly (or randomly) distributed, and which can never generate increasing returns.[10] Manufacturing, with its linked learning (experience) curves, is the passport to wealth generation – and when applied to a solar-hydrogen economy, it is the passport to a post-fossil fuels economy.

No nasties

Or perhaps I should say fewer nasties than in fossil fuelled industries and declining levels as the circular flow economy expands. A solar-hydrogen economy is built on fundamentally safe foundations. There will be little scope for major occupational health disorders or environmental disasters, as there have been through the entire life of the fossil fuels era. This alternative economy is not based on toxic materials with their deadly particulate emissions nor on the extreme hazards of nuclear power. Its core material and energy vectors are simply hydrogen and water – nothing could (in principle) be safer.

It must be conceded that hydrogen cannot simply be substituted for natural gas or oil or coal without other needed modifications. One danger is that, as with other fuels, combustion of hydrogen in air results in the production of nitrogen oxides – another technical challenge to be confronted. Other hazards might also present themselves. And of course, hydrogen is a flammable gas and so sensible precautions will always have to be taken – but its flammability is inferior to that of gasoline or petrol.[11] These issues reveal that the evolution of industry towards a hydrogen basis will need to circumvent several technical issues along the way. These problems will only be overcome if there are sufficiently bold visions for decarbonizing heavy-emissions industrial processes and creating hydrogen-sourced alternatives.

---

10 In our article in *Futures* journal (2014), Erik Reinert and I used the fact that mining and extractive industries suffer from diminishing returns as the basis for the supersession of fossil fuels by renewables. Jeremy Rifkin developed a parallel argument along these lines in his 2002 book on the prospective hydrogen economy.

11 Hydrogen can be explosive in combination with oxygen at concentrations between 18 and 59 per cent – whereas gasoline (petrol) can be explosive in combination with oxygen at much lower concentrations between 1 and 3 per cent. This makes gasoline much more flammable/explosive for any given concentration in air than hydrogen.

Clean energy

A solar-hydrogen economy embodies a clean break from the fossil fuels era.[12] As this alternative economy expands, and fossil fuels contract, so the world becomes less and less polluted by carbon emissions, until they can be expected to dwindle to net zero – by perhaps 2040 or 2050 at the latest. If nuclear is viewed as an alternative low-carbon energy source, it is eminently unsuitable because of its potential dangers. These became manifest in the Russo-Ukraine war of 2022 where Russian bombardment of nuclear reactors in Ukrainian territory triggered potentially catastrophic radiation leakages threatening Europe. By contrast, no one would see bombardment of solar panels as a useful tactic to spread terror in war. A solar-hydrogen economy tends to be safe and reproducible – which is entirely appropriate for an economy with the acronym SHE.

Sustainability

A solar-hydrogen economy is essentially renewable and self-sustaining – unlike its fossil fuels predecessor. It is based on renewables as a source of green hydrogen secured via electrolysis of water, which endlessly restores itself in the global water cycle. The contrast with fossil fuels with their peaking trends and endless price upheavals could not be starker. Whereas renewables as sources of electric power run into problems of intermittency and curtailment, these fluctuations are evened out by storing the energy generated as hydrogen. It behaves like a commodity – just like oil. The green hydrogen generated is both a fuel and a store of energy and a green input to multiple industrial processes, making renewability the signature of an alternative solar-hydrogen economy. Green hydrogen based on electrolysis of water inserts itself in a vast terrestrial water cycle that endlessly renews itself. It represents the achievement of the goal of embedding the economy in renewable natural cycles.

Scalability

The truly fundamental issue involved in the transition to a solar-hydrogen energy system is its scalability, based on its foundation in manufacturing. Can it be scaled to the same level at which fossil fuels operate, with their vast systems for extracting the fuel (drilling for oil or gas, digging for coal),

---

12 There is a case for equating the fossil fuels era with what is now called the Anthropocene – the 'human-made' geological era which is generally considered as starting with the innovation of Newcomen's steam engine in 1712.

transporting it in tankers and rail and through pipelines, refining it, and transporting it again in tankers to the point of use, either chemical plants or heavy engineering plant or petrol/gas stations? Complementing this physical infrastructure is a vast institutional and financial infrastructure that enables the whole system to operate. This is an enormous industrial cum financial system that has been assembled over a century and more, and one that has made the industrialized countries wealthy beyond the dreams of its founders – but is now threatening the planet and our survival as a species through its impact on global warming and other deleterious effects. How can an alternative solar-hydrogen system be scaled up to replace it?

Indeed, the question cannot be evaded: can a solar-hydrogen system be scaled up to act as a substitute for the existing fossil fuelled system, in a reasonable time frame of years rather than decades? Let us break this process down to four steps.

a) Water electrolysis – starting point of a solar-hydrogen economy
b) Can manufacturing be the source of global energy production?
c) Can the scaling up be driven by manufacturing cost reductions?
d) Can the material requirements be satisfied?

Water Electrolysis: Starting Point of the Solar-Hydrogen Economy

The starting point for the solar-hydrogen economy is water electrolysis – the splitting of water into its constituent elements hydrogen and oxygen by an electric current.[13] The process has been known for nearly as long as the recognition of hydrogen and has evolved through alkaline electrolysis cells (currently the most cost-effective) and polymer electrolysis cells, involving a polymer electrolytic membrane, that is a solid-state cell. There is intensive research being conducted in industry and in government research laboratories to improve these tested technologies.[14]

The energy productivity of hydrogen generation via electrolysis is a key consideration. Commercially available electrolytic cells produce hydrogen at an energy cost of around 53 kWh per kg of hydrogen, where 47.5 kWh/kg is consumed in the cell itself and another 5.5 kWh/kg is consumed by

---

13 Because of its reactivity, hydrogen is not freely available; this is why it has to be generated from sources such as water via electrolysis.

14 The book by Marco Alvera` (2021) on the hydrogen revolution has an interesting account of the origins of the complementary technologies of electrolyzer (electric current in water → hydrogen) and fuel cell (hydrogen → electric current).

the apparatus ('balance of plant').[15] The latest capillary-fed electrolysis (CFE) plant developed at the University of Wollongong and the spin-off company Hysata has dramatically improved the energy efficiency of water electrolysis.[16] The estimated required total of 4 Gt hydrogen would be produced using this CFE technology by 44 TW of renewable power/electrolyzer capacity – a dramatic reduction on the 56 TW estimated for current incumbent processes.[17]

This CFE technological breakthrough is the first in several decades to promise a dramatic improvement in the energy productivity of water electrolysis, the foundation of the solar-hydrogen economy. Continued improvement in the energy productivity of water electrolysis, via CFE and beyond, becomes a key focus of the competitive dynamics of the emergent green hydrogen economy.

To those who might argue that the energy cost of producing billions of tonnes of green hydrogen would exceed the energy made available by the use of the hydrogen, there is a clear response. The production of green hydrogen involves first the generation of renewable power in supplying the electricity needed for electrolysis. The scale of generation of renewable power can be increased indefinitely, in keeping with the scale of hydrogen usage in industry, transport and electrification. The green hydrogen will be utilized in specific activities like green steel production or green long-haul heavy transport, calling for the generation of hydrogen via electrolysis utilizing renewable power. There will be no physical limit on the green hydrogen needed or supplied. The declining cost of green hydrogen production, along with declining costs of renewable power, promises to accelerate the shift away from fossil fuels.

---

15 See Hodges et al (2022) for description of the novel capillary-fed electrolysis (CFE) cell.

16 Conventional incumbent electrolyzers operating at 75 per cent efficiency need 14 GW of renewable power/electrolyzer capacity (generating 52.5 kWh per kg hydrogen) to produce 1 million tonnes (1 Mt) green hydrogen per year. The latest Hysata CFE cell, as reported in the peer-reviewed journal *Nature Communications* in March 2022, operates at 95 per cent efficiency and needs only 11 GW of renewable power (electrolyzer capacity) generating 41.5 kWh for the same output of 1 Mt green hydrogen.

17 Note how the argument here moves between the energy content of a given mass of hydrogen and the electrical energy needed via electrolysis to produce that quantity of hydrogen from water. The discussion calls on standards as elaborated in the recent contributions of Lamy and Millet (2020) and by the aforementioned Hodges et al (2022). My thanks to Prof Swiegers for his clarification of these issues.

Focus on manufacturing as means of producing a global hydrogen energy system

The whole point of the solar-hydrogen economy is that it promises to decouple the global energy system from traditional practices of mining, drilling or otherwise extracting fossil fuels. Instead, energy is produced through the use of manufactured devices – electrolyzers, solar panels, wind turbines, batteries and FCEVs – that are all products of manufacturing and subject to engineering design. And manufacturing is not just a source of wealth; it is essentially available to all.

In the case of a solar-hydrogen economy, I argue above that green hydrogen would be needed at a scale of 4 billion tonnes per year (4 Gt/y) if it is to substitute for nearly 500 EJ of energy from fossil fuels in their entirety. There is no hiding the fact that this is a colossal transformation. But precisely because it can be manufactured (i.e. generated through manufactured devices, namely electrolyzers), this is a practicable engineering challenge and one that can (in principle) be met. It would have to be met in stages as it is ramped up, and not in a single, sudden transformation.

The production of 500 EJ of green hydrogen in a year would call for an electrolyzer capacity of 44 trillion watts (44 TW) at the current best commercial levels of energy productivity using capillary flow electrolysis.[18] Now current electrolyzer capacity reached around 0.3 GW in 2020 – giving a sense of how vastly the manufacturing systems needed for the eventual hydrogen economy need to be scaled up.[19] But the problems are simply technical in character – they do not call for miracles.

Manufacturing thus provides the key to the practicability of the creation of a solar-hydrogen economy – and a means of estimating the scale of the system needed to replace fossil fuels in their entirety. And manufacturing itself generates the driver for its further expansion because of cost reductions.

Continuing manufacturing cost reductions: learning curves

We can be confident that costs for water electrolysis and other aspects of the solar-hydrogen economy will continue to fall – not in a random and haphazard fashion

---

18 Note that the new electrolyzer technology of capillary flow electrolysis (CFE) improves energy productivity from 56 TW down to 44 TW needed to produce 500 EJ of green hydrogen.

19 See the IEA (2021) report on hydrogen for the 0.3 GW figure. So 56 GW would be 150 times that level, 56 TW would be 1000 times larger, or 150,000 – a vast scaling up, but technically achievable.

(as with fossil fuels) but in a systematic fashion driven by the learning curve for each technology. Learning curves depict cost reductions associated with all manufacturing activities. This is the basis of the increasing returns associated with all manufacturing – as recognized by economists going back to the seventeenth century in Italy.[20] It is because a solar-hydrogen system is based on manufactured products (PV cells, electrolyzers) that we can count on its costs declining – as a result of competitive innovations and up-scaling (market expansion).

The record for cost reduction in manufactured energy products is clear – solar PV, wind turbines and batteries. Consider the case of lithium-ion batteries, where the cost declines over the past three decades have been emphatic, due to the combined effects of the learning curve and market expansion (Figure 1).[21]

The chart reveals a 97 per cent cost decline since 1991. Note that this has nothing to do with the cost of mined lithium, which has actually been rising as demand intensifies due to the impact of battery electric vehicles.[22] The cost decline is entirely due to the manufacturing aspects – the learning (experience) curve and the scale of production effect, which together overwhelm the rising price of the mined lithium product. Here we have the fundamental attribute

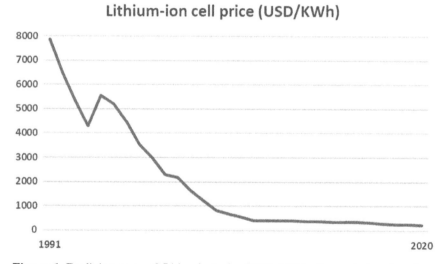

Figure 1 Declining costs of Li-ion batteries (1991–2020). *Source:* Author based on data from MIT.

---

20 See Reinert (2016) on Antonio Serra, *Short Treatise on the Wealth and Poverty of Nations* (1613).

21 See MIT study by Ziegler and Trancik (2021).

22 See Lithium price rise: Electric vehicle demand leads to record surge | news.com.au.

that distinguishes green hydrogen from its multi-coloured competitors. It is the declining costs associated with the manufacturing learning curves that are linked to generating hydrogen from water via electrolysis using renewable power and to subsequent processes that are the drivers of the new system's propagation. The renewables themselves are declining in cost with the learning (experience) curve. The electrolyzers are declining in cost as the market expands and the learning curve kicks in. And the subsequent processes like green steel production, or green cement or green ammonia fertilizers would likewise be declining in cost.

This whole system is thus a *triple-powered cost decline process* that can be expected to overwhelm any cost increase induced in mining operations and geopolitical developments like wars and revolutions and puts the countries and firms that pin their strategies to green hydrogen on the right side of history.

Material requirements: circularity

Manufacturing depends on inputs of raw materials, which are frequently identified as setting limits to the expansion of the green economy. But increasingly these materials are being sourced from circular flows (recycling, urban mining) rather than from one-off commodity inputs sourced from mining or extraction. While rare earths are routinely discussed as material 'barriers' to the green transition, in reality they are becoming less and less important as more of the flows are sourced from the circular economy. As a solar-hydrogen economy takes hold, its dependence on freshly mined or extracted commodities promises to decline as the circular economy expands.[23]

'Urban mining' is the apposite term for the extraction of materials not from the earth but from circular flows of manufactured products.[24] Whole cities are envisaged as practitioners of materials recycling and 'urban mining' that can be expected to increasingly take over from mining as extraction of materials from the earth – whether drilling for oil or gas or mining for raw materials like iron ore, lithium or bauxite. The green hydrogen industrial revolution with its dependence on a global water cycle promises to play its

---

23 The argument being presented does not depend on the circular economy becoming the norm rather than the exception as currently holds. But the grand cycle of water and hydrogen in the solar hydrogen economy promises to give a powerful impetus to circularity generally. Of course, certain aspects of recovering minerals from manufactured parts may prove recalcitrant, but they will present less of a problem as other materials come to be derived from circular flows.

24 See my article on urban mining in the China e-waste industry, completed with my Chinese colleagues Xianlai Zeng and Jinhui Li (Zeng, Mathews and Li 2018).

part in driving the swing away from dependence on materials extracted from the earth with their increasing costs and declining returns.

Competitive Dynamics of Emergence of the Green Hydrogen Economy

Moving on from the technical issues that set limits to the generation of hydrogen and its flow along multiple pathways through the economy, we confront the business and economic issues that will drive and shape the transition. Central to this perspective will be the role to be played by the extant oil companies. Some will grasp the opportunities created by the green hydrogen transition and redeploy their capabilities and expertise in managing large flows of fossil fuels to managing large flows of green hydrogen. But others will no doubt seek to extend the life of their investments in fossil fuels infrastructure and attempt to block the transition to green hydrogen – by fair means or otherwise.

Take the Information Technology sector as a case where we know that a fundamental transition took place from the dominance of mainframe computers in the early 1980s to the technological revolution instigated by the personal computer (PC). The big mainframes with all their ancillary systems were produced by companies such as IBM, AT&T, Wang Laboratories and Digital Equipment; these companies had the money, leadership, skills and potential motivation to lead the PC revolution. But instead some disappeared, some fell from leadership positions and none defined the new market – which was instead created by the upstarts Microsoft, Apple and Intel. This experience reinforces the perception that the history of business disruption and market transition suggests that legacy companies rarely lead the way or usher in a transition to a new regime.

There is certainly plenty of evidence that legacy oil companies (as well as coal and gas companies) are actively seeking to block the green transition. Companies like Exxon are actively promoting the continuation of oil drilling activities as well as the extension of pipeline infrastructure, while their activities in international forums to block moves to penalize carbon emissions are amply documented.[25] But the energy transition is remarkable in that several oil companies are already deeply involved in the green hydrogen transition, while countries in East Asia are driving their firms to embrace the green transition and adopt leadership positions in the competitive dynamics that are emerging.

---

25 See for example Jeremy Leggett's accounts in successive works on the climate and oil wars (2018).

Indeed it is remarkable how the green hydrogen industrial revolution promises to involve oil companies in a progressive way with the energy transition. The oil companies are the extant fossil fuel system behemoths. They were not involved in the development of renewable energies at the outset (with some exceptions like Total in wind and BP in solar) nor in the creation of the circular economy – but the shift to green hydrogen gives them an opportunity to become players in the future energy system, alongside small entrepreneurial specialists in hydrogen production, storage, distribution and usage. And the oil companies are the masters of scale.

Oil company involvement

Already some oil majors are using their expertise in offshore oil platforms to transition to offshore wind power generation – like Equinor in Norway. This is indeed a sensible diversification to be adopted by oil majors. Hydrogen generation – its production, storage, transport (via e.g. pipelines) and distribution as fuel – is much closer to oil company business models than renewables (such as offshore wind power). Smart oil companies will place themselves at the forefront of the transition. This does not mean supporting 'blue' hydrogen (sourced from methane or natural gas) as an alternative to 'green' because that option leaves the oil majors stranded in a world of fossil fuels. Rather it means oil companies embracing the vast infrastructure needed for the green hydrogen revolution and managing the transition at scale, in all its physical and financial complexity – something that the oil majors definitely know how to manage.

Both BP as a leading Western oil giant and Sinopec as the leading Chinese oil giant are involved in making extensive investments in the green hydrogen economy – thus pointing to where they see their own future and to likely imitation by other fossil fuel leaders. In June 2022, BP announced that it was taking a 40.5 per cent share in a huge green hydrogen hub in Western Australia, becoming the largest shareholder in the Asian Renewable Energy Hub (AREH) and taking over responsibility for operating the project – a major diversification for BP away from owning and operating oil projects. The AREH is based on vast solar and wind farms in the remote Pilbara region of Western Australia, totalling 26 GW of renewable power; the stated ambition of the $36 billion project is to build a 10 per cent share of the global green hydrogen market.[26]

---

26 See 'Oil giant BP swoops for largest stake in $36 bn green hydrogen mega-project in Australia', *Recharge*, 15 June 2022, at: Oil giant BP swoops for largest stake in $36bn green hydrogen mega-project in Australia | Recharge (rechargenews.com).

For its part, Sinopec announced in May 2022 that it would invest heavily in projects involving the production of green hydrogen and the manufacture of hydrogen electrolyzers, beginning with a project in China's Xinjiang province to produce 52 alkaline-based hydrogen electrolyzers. The first part of the project, involving as contractors Belgium's John Cockerill and two Chinese firms, and calling for an investment of 1.07 billion yuan (US$160 million), was announced in May 2022.[27] This confirms that Sinopec is taking active steps to become China's leading green hydrogen producer and user, building on other investments such as green chemicals based on green hydrogen feedstock.

The involvement of both BP and Sinopec in an emerging green hydrogen industry gives the lie to claims that oil majors would forever be opposed to the green transition and would effectively block it completely. Indeed the reality is that smart oil companies like BP and Sinopec can see the writing on the wall and can envisage a green hydrogen future for themselves, setting a precedent that will no doubt be followed by many others. The more that existing fossil fuel or commodity companies become involved in green hydrogen (like oil companies BP or Sinopec or other fossil fuel giants like iron ore producer Fortescue Metals in Australia or Reliance in India), the more they perceive the opportunities involved and become motivated to lead the transition – with all their financial and organizational clout.[28] It is a transition best described as a circular and cumulative process – or an instance of circular and cumulative causation. This perspective, long marginalized in economic reasoning, should now come to the fore in describing and analyzing the green hydrogen shift.

'Total Substitution' Perspective

It cannot be emphasized enough that the success of the green hydrogen transition depends on achieving vast economies of scale. What is needed is what I call a 'total substitution' perspective – where green hydrogen is viewed as potentially being able to substitute for *all fossil fuel uses* and applications in

---

27 See 'Sinopec selects contractors for world's largest solar-to-hydrogen project', by Xu Yihe, *Upstream*, 17 May 2022, at: Sinopec selects contractors for world's largest solar-to-hydrogen project | Upstream Online.

28 It was the absence of oil companies from the renewables revolution that was always its Achilles heel – now potentially remedied by the turn towards the green hydrogen economy.

their entirety.[29] We are talking about investments of trillions of dollars in terawatts of renewable power to produce billions of tonnes of liquid hydrogen (and derivatives like ammonia) in a vast energy system that can drive the entire industrial economy.

Of course, this does not mean that hydrogen has to substitute for fossil fuels in every single activity – merely that it has to have the potential to do so. Many of the processes where fossil fuels are currently utilized can be electrified – as is obviously the case with electric vehicles – but can also be achieved with domestic heating or recycling of materials. Electrification can in this way also be viewed as the modernization of industry and as a complement to the use of hydrogen, rolling back dependence on fossil fuels. Electrification is a rising trend – reaching 20 per cent of global final energy consumption in 2020.[30] As it rises it reduces the necessity for substitution by green hydrogen – which can be focused on such 'hard to reach' processes as steel or cement or glass production.

I argued above that the scale in energetic terms of the incumbent fossil fuels system reaches 500 EJ per year in its entirety, and a comparable level in terms of hydrogen would potentially call for the production of 4 billion tonnes of green hydrogen (4 Gt/y), via electrolysis, which would in turn call for a maximum of 44 TW of electrolyzer capacity – at the energy productivity of the new CFE cells. This is the outer limit of the substitution process. I mention these vast sums to emphasize the potential scale of substitution needed – but also to emphasize how the substitution is eminently achievable over the course of the next several years and decades, as the scale of manufacturing is built up. Green hydrogen would be introduced sequentially in one industrial sector after another, in a self-reinforcing process best captured in the heterodox economic expression 'circular and cumulative causation'.

If the world can produce and refine 4.5 billion tonnes of oil every year, investing $2.6 trillion in the process, then we can certainly produce 4 billion tonnes of green hydrogen each year, from manufactured electrolyzers reaching a capacity of more than 40 TW (trillion watts), calling for huge investments at the scale of trillions of dollars.[31] In the earlier years of the transition, say over the next 5 to 10 years (2023–2028 and 2033), we would expect to

---

29 There is by now a growing literature on the feasibility of an energy system powered 100 per cent by renewables. For a recent overview, see Breyer et al (2022).

30 See Enerdata, 'Share of electricity in total final energy consumption' at: Share of electricity in total final energy consumption (enerdata.net).

31 Goldman Sachs in their 2022 report *The Clean Hydrogen Revolution* posits that US$5 trillion in cumulative investments in the clean hydrogen supply chain will be required for net zero. See Carbonomics: The Clean Hydrogen Revolution (goldmansachs.com).

see modest gains in the development of new green hydrogen value chains, along with end uses such as FCEVs and the infrastructure needed to promote them. Phased transition can also be expected in hydrogen-powered shipping (again utilizing fuel calls) with bunkers for the supply of green hydrogen in leading ports like Shanghai, Shenzhen or Ningbo-Zhoushan in China, or Los Angeles, Long Beach or New York in the United States, or Hamburg, Rotterdam and Antwerp in Europe. Purely market-based competitive dynamics would not be expected to drive the transition fast enough, but if market dynamics combined with state leadership and state-owned enterprise is envisaged (as is increasingly the case in China and East Asia) then the transition might just be accomplished in time to avert the worst aspects of global warming. Patience in making the transition in stages is needed, to ensure that the green hydrogen paradigm might successfully supersede the fossil fuels paradigm.

Where would the funds for such a momentous change come from? I and many others have been pointing to the need to move beyond public finances (based ultimately on taxation) in effecting the green shift. Instead, this transition calls for the mechanisms of the capital markets – the $50 trillion global equity markets, and the twice as large $100 trillion bond markets (debt capital). The NGO Climate Bonds Initiative (CBI) has been tracking the emergence of climate mitigation-focused bond issues and their uptake by bonds investors. By 2021, the global green bonds market was worth $0.5 trillion – still a relatively small quantum but one that indicates what is possible. The cumulative level of green bonds issued up to 2021 was $1.5 trillion. The CBI is predicting that green bonds will hit $1 trillion in issuance by 2022, and $5 trillion by 2025.[32] These are the markets where major industrialists are likely to find the funds needed to invest in their grand plans for promoting the green hydrogen industrial revolution.

The CBI has been tracking and analysing the emergence and maturation of the green bonds market, following the progress of issuances, offering standards that define green bonds and promoting the concept of capital debt markets financing the green transition. Now as the world approaches the advent of the solar-hydrogen economy, the necessity for trillion-dollar investments in green hydrogen by both governments and private entrepreneurs will become obvious.

---

32 See *Climate Bonds Market Intelligence* 2021, 31 January 2022, at: $500bn Green Issuance 2021: social and sustainable acceleration: Annual green $1tn in sight: Market expansion forecasts for 2022 and 2025 | Climate Bonds Initiative.

One of the reasons for insisting that the transition to a solar-hydrogen economy calls for a green industrial revolution, involving multiple industrial transitions, is that these shifts promise to provide multiple opportunities for entrepreneurs to invest in new steps in value chains and new linkages between value chains, in a complex of processes that can only be described as an industrial revolution. What then will this green industrial revolution look like? Where will the new opportunities for investment appear? We turn now to examine the multiple pathways traced by green hydrogen in the process of substituting one industrial system for another.

Chapter 3

MULTIPLE GREEN HYDROGEN PATHWAYS

The attractive feature of the green industrial revolution is that it involves multiple pathways, starting with green hydrogen itself (from renewably powered electrolysis of water) and then tracing the hydrogen through multiple transitions – involving such industries as green steel, or other green metals like aluminium, to green cement, or green glass or green fertilizers producing green food.[1] The end step in each pathway involves hydrogen being 'burnt' to produce water again, in a grand global cycle. All of these pathways involve one or more steps where green hydrogen can substitute for carbon – as coal/coke, gas or oil. These carbon-intensive pathways have in common that as heavy users of carbon they are also high carbon emitters – in their present form. This is where the hydrogen economy really has the potential to make its mark.

Take the steel industry. It took several steps for the modern open hearth steel furnace to arrive, involving the development of a furnace to produce cast iron in the early nineteenth century and then a 'puddling' furnace to produce wrought iron and finally the innovation of the blast furnace introduced by Henry Bessemer in 1856 which used a blast of hot air to remove impurities to produce steel. The blast furnace utilizes coke (coal heated in the absence of air) as a means of introducing carbon as a reducing agent, and so the levels of carbon emissions are correspondingly (impossibly) high – so high that the steel industry was thought to be an intractable source of industrial carbon emissions. Further innovations have seen the introduction of the electric arc furnace (EAF) and the capacity to utilize recycled steel ('scrap steel') as

---

1 Note that 'green aluminium' generally refers to aluminium produced from bauxite (mostly aluminium oxide) at high temperatures achieved in an electric furnace, using green power (usually hydropower). See: 'Green aluminium maker sees opportunity in green hydrogen', *Bloomberg News*, 24 July 2020, at: Green aluminium maker sees opportunity in hydrogen - MINING.COM.

raw material – but the fundamentals of the process remain based on carbon. What if hydrogen could be introduced at scale to take over from coke in the smelting of iron and the production of steel?

Other metals likewise are produced by smelting from their mineral ores at high temperatures – such as aluminium or copper or tin. In all these cases, the high temperatures are secured through heating with coke (carbon) which acts as both a heat source and reactant. What if hydrogen could be introduced in place of carbon?

Cement is another carbon-intensive heavy industrial process that displays what has appeared to be an irreducible level of high carbon emissions. When combined with sand and aggregate, cement forms concrete, which is far and away the world's principal building material. Cement was one of the great innovations of the Romans, who found a naturally occurring mineral called pozzolana that could be set under water (and so was used extensively by the Romans in building their aqueducts). The modern synthetic counterpart of pozzolana is Portland cement, which is produced in a cement kiln from limestone (calcium carbonate) and clay (containing various silicates) heated to and fused at very high temperatures. High temperatures are achieved using fossil fuel combustion. What if the burning of hydrogen (with water as the end product) could be used to achieve a similar high temperature?

Then there are fertilizers, mostly based on ammonia as a source of the nitrogen needed by plants. Ammonia is a combination of nitrogen and hydrogen (NH_3) and is produced at a vast industrial scale by the Haber-Bosch (HB) process – a process of 'fixing' nitrogen from the air and blending it with hydrogen under conditions of high temperature and pressure and in the presence of metallic catalysts. The HB process was one of the great industrial innovations of the twentieth century, introduced during wartime conditions by the German chemists Fritz Haber and Carl Bosch, and characterized with little exaggeration as the primary industrial process on which our entire industrial civilization depends.[2] The hydrogen utilized in HB ammonia production is almost always sourced from steam reformation of methane (natural gas). What if green hydrogen were utilized instead and alternative pathways needing lower temperatures could be devised?

The point of mentioning these various industrial processes such as the production of green steel or cement or ammonia is that these processes lie at the very core of our industrial civilization and are responsible, as heavy industry,

---

2 See Smil (2004) for the definitive account of the origins and influence of the Haber-Bosch process for producing synthetic ammonia.

for an overwhelming majority of carbon emissions. How are these processes to be decarbonized by substituting hydrogen?[3]

Green Hydrogen Industrial Processes

There are by now several practical demonstrations that hydrogen can replace carbon in high temperature, heavy industrial processes including steel, cement, glass, chemicals or fertilizers. It is not technology so much as industrial will that is the principal barrier. This is where grand industrial visions where states set goals and industrialists can follow through and make a decisive difference. Let us go through the various pathways involved in creating a solar-hydrogen economy, focusing on industries that require high temperatures which are achieved currently through the combustion of fossil fuels or heating by electric current.[4]

Green steel

Steel is the product of high-temperature smelting of iron ore with controlled carbon content introduced into a blast furnace as coke, which is coal heated in the absence of air. The blast furnace, introduced by British inventor Henry Bessemer in 1856, is one of the iconic images of the industrial revolution – and now one of the most stubborn sources of high carbon emissions. Steel companies have made progress in reducing emissions by producing steel in EAFs using rising levels of recycled steel as scrap. And a further reduction in emissions involves introducing natural gas as a partial substitute for coke, to produce direct reduced iron. Many steel producers have embarked on these improvements. But what about introducing hydrogen?

In the European Union (EU), steel producers like Arcelor-Mittal, Voestalpine (Austria) and SSAB (Sweden) as well the German giant Thyssenkrupp have announced tentative investment steps to switch to hydrogen as input. Thyssenkrupp, which operates the largest steel plant in Europe

---

3 For recent reviews of the industrial pathways through which green hydrogen may be introduced, see for example Oliveira et al (2021) or Eljack and Kazi (2021). I argue below that this is the principal reason why green hydrogen may be considered as a general-purpose technology, driving a new techno-economic surge.

4 Hydrogen burns at just over 2000 degrees C in air – at 2030 degrees C in fact. See 'Flame temperatures Table for different fuels', *ThoughtCo.*, at: Typical Flame Temperature for Different Fuels (thoughtco.com).

in Duisberg, is actively experimenting with the use of green hydrogen as a reducing agent.[5]

In Sweden, there is a strong push by an industry consortium HyBrIT (Hydrogen Breakthrough Ironmaking Technology) to eliminate carbon from the steelmaking process altogether. While pilot operations are still in progress, already there is a Swedish steel company H2 Green Steel which has announced plans to forge a green steel plant – building on the prior steps of the HyBrIT project. Founded in 2020, the company announced its goal of producing steel in a fully integrated greenfield plant in Boden, utilizing green electricity and green hydrogen. A second green hydrogen plant is being built in Spain in a JV with Spanish energy giant Iberdrola.[6]

The real test for green steel is likely to come from China and India, now the world's two largest steel producers and correspondingly the world's largest carbon emitters from their steel production processes. It can be anticipated that these countries will surprise the world with the speed of their transition, once the decarbonization pathway is clear.[7] On the other hand, it is highly likely that major fossil fuels exporters may seize the opportunity to diversify to become processing superpowers utilizing green hydrogen – such as Australia.[8]

Green cement

Cement production is one of the most intensive carbon-using and carbon-emitting industrial processes. In the nineteenth century, the innovation of Portland cement was introduced, involving high-temperature breakdown of naturally found products like calcium carbonates and silicates and their fusing to form new materials in the cement kiln. Cement producers are now starting to experiment with ways of introducing green hydrogen into the process in order to achieve the high temperatures required.

---

5 See 'Thyssenkrupp presents plan for carbon-neutral steel plant', *Reuters*, 28 August 2020, at: Thyssenkrupp presents plan for carbon neutral steel plant | Reuters.

6 See 'Producing green steel in a fully integrated, digitalised and automated Greenfield steel plant', H2 Green Steel, at: Producing green steel in a fully integrated, digitalized and automated Greenfield steel plant. — H2 Green Steel.

7 See 'Climate change: Technology key to decarbonisation of Chinese steel mills, BHP executive says', by Eric Ng, 20 Feb 2022, *South China Morning Post*, at: Climate Change: technology key to decarbonisation of Chinese steel mills, BHP executive says | South China Morning Post (scmp.com).

8 The most recent book by economist Prof Ross Garnaut (2019) makes this very argument.

Some of the cement giants are seeking to find a way of introducing green hydrogen into the cement-making process. In the UK, Heidelberg Cement for example is experimenting with ground granulated blast furnace slag (which when ground can substitute for cement) where hydrogen is utilized in place of coke.[9] Again, China as the world's largest producer of cement is anticipated to play a critical role in the coming transition.[10]

Green glass

Glass is another industrial product where traditional methods employ high levels of carbon and consequently high levels of carbon emissions. Some breakthroughs have been reported. In August 2021, UK glassmaker Pilkington announced that it had replaced natural gas with hydrogen at its float glass (sheet glass) factory at St Helens, in Liverpool. The project is part of the UK government-led Hydrogen Strategy, *HyNet Industrial Fuel Switching* project, with the hydrogen being supplied by BOC.[11]

Green plastics

Plastics producers like Covestro (that manufactures polyurethane and polycarbamate products) are now turning to green hydrogen as a substitute feedstock. Covestro, based in the industrial city Leverkusen (Germany), produces high-tech polymer materials, including polyurethanes and polycarbamates. In January 2022, Covestro announced that it had agreed to purchase green hydrogen from Australian producer Fortescue Future Industries (FFI). The deal is for FFI to supply Covestro with up to 100,000 tonnes GH_2 per year, starting in 2024, for input into the company's production plants in Europe, Asia and North America. Covestro has since announced that it would be producing plastic products at its Shanghai factory utilizing green hydrogen.[12]

---

9   See 'Cement giants turn to green hydrogen, carbon capture to curb emissions', by Anmar Frangoul, *CNBC*, 15 February 2021, at: Cement giants turn to green hydrogen, carbon capture to curb emissions (cnbc.com).

10 See 'Hydrogen seen as green way forward', by Zheng Xin, *China Daily*, 6 February 2021, at: Hydrogen seen as green way forward - Chinadaily.com.cn.

11 See '"World first" as hydrogen used to manufacture glass', by Kelvin Ross, *Power Engineering International*, 26 August 2021, at: 'World first' as hydrogen used to manufacture glass - Power Engineering International.

12 See 'Covestro plans to use green hydrogen to make mattresses, water barrels more sustainable', *Hydrogen Central*, 9 February 2022, at: Covestro Plans to use Green Hydrogen to Make Mattresses, Water Barrels More Sustainable – Hydrogen Central (hydrogen-central.com).

Green aluminium

Aluminium production utilizes high levels of electric power needed to attain the high temperatures required. One path to greening involves utilizing green electric power – solar, wind or hydropower. Now industrial giants like Rio Tinto are engaged in R&D projects to investigate the introduction of hydrogen directly into the aluminium production process such as at the Yarwun alumina refinery in Gladstone (Qld). Projects like Rio's partnerships with the Australian Renewable Energy Agency and Sumitomo Corporation are already underway.[13]

Green fertilizers → green food

There are many pathways that involve green hydrogen culminating in food production. Ammonia is a chemical combination of nitrogen and hydrogen (NH_3) and is the major constituent of fertilizers which stimulate plant growth by making the nitrogen available. (It cannot be taken up by plants in gaseous form.) Currently ammonia is generally made by producing hydrogen from natural gas, and nitrogen from air using an air separation unit, and the two elements are then combined via the HB process (calling for high temperatures and pressures as well as expensive metallic catalysts).[14] Green ammonia could become a major export item as the green transition evolves.

Green Hydrogen-Propelled Transport

> Fuel cell vehicles are mind-bogglingly stupid
>
> —Elon Musk[15]

While this chapter focuses on the major industrial pathways traced by green hydrogen in the solar-hydrogen economy, there are of course well-known transport initiatives where hydrogen can also be expected to play a role as a major substitute for oil and fossil fuels. Not everyone agrees with this

---

13 See 'Rio Tinto and Sumitomo to assess hydrogen pilot plant at Gladstone's Yarwun alumina refinery', *GreenCarCongress*, 25 August 2021, at: Rio Tinto and Sumitomo to assess hydrogen pilot plant at Gladstone's Yarwun alumina refinery – Green Car Congress.

14 The Australian government (via ARENA) is supporting the building of a prototype green ammonia facility operated jointly by Yara Pilbara and Engie, with a grant of A$42.5 million. See Yara webpage, at: Green ammonia | Yara Australia.

15 Elon Musk in January 2014; see for example: Tesla CEO Elon Musk: Hydrogen Fuel Cell Vehicles Are 'Mind-Bogglingly Stupid' (insideevs.com).

perspective – as the quote from Elon Musk exemplifies. As a major producer of battery-powered electric vehicles (BEVs), Musk of course has a stake in dismissing the competing technology of fuel cell-powered electric vehicles (FCEVs). His point is that why use electricity to produce hydrogen from water only to 'burn' the hydrogen in fuel cells to produce electricity again, this time to drive an electric motor in a vehicle. If the battle were confined to passenger vehicles, then BEVs vs FCEVs would doubtless go the BEVs' way – to the chagrin of Toyota which has been backing FCEVs all the way.

The real point is that batteries are good stores of energy only up to a certain size. For anything larger than a small passenger vehicle – say buses, or vans, or trucks, and then up to trains, or boats and ships – the battery as a store of energy becomes less and less practicable, taking up more and more of the volume in the vehicle or vessel as well as more of the weight, and green hydrogen used with fuel cells instead becomes increasingly attractive. Hence there have been numerous commercial initiatives involving substituting internal combustion engines as well as external combustion engines (burning diesel) by FCs fuelled by green hydrogen.[16]

For shipping the promise of hydrogen-fuelled propulsion using fuel cells is enormous, and several cases of commercial initiatives such as cruise liners are now reported. The most arresting of these initiatives is that of the *Energy Observer*, a floating laboratory vessel that draws seawater from around the boat to produce hydrogen via filtration and electrolysis and then drives a fuel cell from Toyota to power a marine engine.[17] What is so attractive about this concept is that it taps a limitless supply of water to produce a limitless supply of hydrogen, all without any carbon pollution.

Another frontier in hydrogen-fuelled transport is that of hydrogen as a combustible fuel to be fed into turbines in aircraft – as being presently explored by Airbus and other aircraft manufacturers. These and other initiatives are described in the current business reports on green hydrogen such as Goldman Sachs' *The clean hydrogen revolution*.[18] Then there are applications of hydrogen as thermal fuel in shipping and aviation, in addition to its use as fuel for the generation of electricity via fuel cells in motorized transport (light FCEVs and heavy FCEVs such as buses, trucks and trains). These topics are well-known and widely discussed and do not call for elaboration here.

---

16 See for example results of experiments with fuel cell-powered heavy duty vehicles at Oak Ridge National Laboratory, at: Heavy-duty vehicles an ideal entry into hydrogen fuel cell use | ORNL.

17 See the video report, 'First boat to make its own hydrogen fuel from seawater', at: First boat to make its own hydrogen fuel from seawater – YouTube.

18 See Carbonomics: The Clean Hydrogen Revolution (goldmansachs.com).

Green Hydrogen as Industrial Input Across
Numerous Sectors: Hydrogen Hubs

'It is my belief that the next 1,000 unicorns – companies that have a market valu-
ation over a billion dollars – won't be a search engine, won't be a media company,
they'll be businesses developing green hydrogen, green agriculture, green steel and
green cement'

—Larry Fink, CEO Blackrock[19]

The industrial pathways generated for the diffusion of green hydrogen via
a novel solar-hydrogen industrial system are all well-known and are being
experimented with in a serious way by industrial corporations looking for
alternative ways to make profits and put their business on a sustainable foot-
ing. The vision enunciated by Larry Fink, CEO of the world's largest hedge
fund, Blackrock, is typical of well-informed financial circles. It is the multi-
plicity of the alternative green hydrogen pathways that give the 'total substitution' character to the solar-hydrogen economy. There are possibilities for
numerous entrepreneurial initiatives in introducing new steps in the newly
created value chains. This is the 'creative' aspect of Schumpeter's creative
destruction, with the destructive aspect as the complementary dismantling of
fossil fuel operations where coal or coke or natural gas is used in extant versions of these various heavy industries.

Green hydrogen clusters

The key to driving the propagation of these various green hydrogen-based
industrial processes is to allow firms to capture increasing returns from the
interlinkages created as value chains intersect through entrepreneurial initiatives. And the best way to generate these interlinkages is to create industrial hubs, or clusters, particularly hubs where green hydrogen activities are
favoured. It is in green hubs that value chains can interact and intersect with
each other to generate increasing returns, via chain reactions of such inter-
sections. This is a heterodox economic perspective that goes to the core of
dynamic industrial processes – and is ignored in mainstream economics.

I was invited to sketch out how countries that promote their greening
activities through industrial hubs, or clusters, do better than countries and
regions that leave companies to seek to prosper on their own, in the *Oxford*

---

19 Larry Fink at Middle East Green Initiative Summit, Riyadh, Saudi Arabia, 25 Oct
2021; see: Blackrock CEO Larry Fink: Next 1,000 unicorns will be in climate tech
(cnbc.com).

Handbook on Industrial Hubs and Economic Development, edited by Arkebe Oqubay and Justin Yifu Lin. In my chapter 24 contributed to this handbook, 'The greening of industrial hubs: A 21st century development strategy', I framed an argument along the following lines.

Countries embarked on industrialization programme in the twenty-first century have everything to gain by focusing their strategies on building agglomerations of firms known as industrial parks or hubs or clusters. In these supra-organizational structures firms can generate increasing returns through capturing systemic synergies. If such an organizational strategy is combined with a green growth strategy, where renewables take over from fossil fuels to ensure energy security, the two stand the best chance of success if pursued in industrial hubs, where industrial parks are turned into eco-industrial parks. China is an exemplary case where this strategy is being pursued, where co-location of firms and initiatives to capture joint efficiency effects (through shared resources and inputs) are pursued.[20]

It is clear that the process of building a solar-hydrogen economy will be accelerated and promoted by the deliberate creation of industrial hubs, or eco-industrial parks or clusters. Where these hubs or clusters are created will have an important bearing on the geopolitical dynamics of the propagation of the green hydrogen economy.

International Political Economy of Green Hydrogen Competitive Dynamics

The evolution of the green hydrogen economy is likely to be driven not just by technical considerations but by competitive dynamics principally between East Asia, North America and Europe. Indeed the green hydrogen industrial revolution promises to be a principal battleground where these competitive dynamics play out. The East Asian countries led by Japan but now dominated by China have already caught up with the West, through judicious use of fast follower state-led strategies of technological leverage, and are now looking to occupy positions of leadership based on practices of innovation rather than imitation.

Spanning several interconnected industrial sectors, the green hydrogen revolution promises to give countries with the longest technological foresight the advantage – and that means that East Asian countries with their

---

20 See Mathews (2020). For a copy of the text of the chapter (reproduced in typescript with permission from the publisher), see Greening of industrial hubs: A 21st century development strategy (globalgreenshift.org).

state-framed strategies of what my colleagues and I call 'developmental environmentalism' will build an advantage.[21]

At this stage, there are few reports of Chinese initiatives in creating solar-hydrogen eco-industrial parks or hubs to focus the development of the country's green economy. But it can be safely predicted that such reports will proliferate in future months and years. Already in March 2022, the Chinese National Development and Reform Commission announced a new target for green hydrogen production of 200,000 tonnes per year by 2025 – by far the highest in the world.[22] Already there are signs that Chinese firms are moving into leadership positions in hydrogen-related industries. The chemicals producer Baofeng, for example, has commenced green hydrogen production from the world's largest plant – a 150 MW alkaline electrolyzer powered by a 200 MW solar array, which came online in late December 2021. It is five times larger than Baofeng's previous record holder. But already the state-owned Sinopec, an oil giant, has broken ground on an even larger 260 MW electrolyzer, due to come online in mid-2023.[23]

South Korea is another East Asian country that has aspirations to establish a national hydrogen economy with strong state support, with promotional policies that span successive administrations. The Korean strategy explicitly views green hydrogen as accounting for 5 per cent of projected power consumption by 2040, as well as major contributions to employment and economic growth (green growth) as well as reductions in particulate emissions to reduce urban pollution and carbon emissions to counter global warming.[24] This is doubtless a trend that other countries will follow.

We can be fairly certain that the United States has already lost its leadership position in the green transition because of attempts to prolong fossil fuel dominance via the innovation of hydraulic fracture ('fracking') which has inevitably overshadowed initiatives designed to break with fossil fuels in favour of renewables and green hydrogen. Meanwhile, the EU continues to generate leading firms in the green transition space, but they remain marginal in the absence of determined efforts to create fresh markets through

---

21 See our forthcoming work *Developmental Environmentalism* by Thurbon, Kim, Tan and Mathews (2023).

22 See 'China targets 200k tonnes of green hydrogen by 2025', 23 March 2022, at: China targets 200k tonnes of green hydrogen by 2025 – Energy Live News.

23 See 'China starts up world's largest green hydrogen plant', *Energy Voice*, 3 February 2022, at: China starts up world's largest green hydrogen plant - News for the Energy Sector (energyvoice.com).

24 See Stangarone (2021) as well as our own case studies of Korean strategies in our forthcoming book *Developmental Environmentalism* (Thurbon, Kim, Tan and Mathews) (2023).

state-mediated activity. It is in these circumstances that business initiatives by industrialists loom as so significant – as in cases like FFI in Australia.

Green Hydrogen Industrialists' Targets

Consider how industrialists are leading the charge in building multiply-intersecting new value chains. Take the case of Fortescue Future Industries (FFI) founded by Australian iron ore magnate Andrew 'Twiggy' Forrest. FFI spun out of Forrest's iron ore mining enterprise Fortescue Mining Group is in the serious business of aiming to be the single largest company in the world promoting the green industrial transformation. FFI, through Forrest, is on record as viewing green hydrogen as the driver of the green transformation, where the green hydrogen economy might be framed as worth $12 trillion or more by 2050 – in less than 30 years. At the current costs of producing green hydrogen from electrolysis of water using renewable electric power, amounting to $1.2 million per MW, that would translate into $1.2 billion per GW, or $1.2 trillion per TW, and $12 trillion as producing 10 TW of green electric power – comparable to the current world scale of the entire fossil fuel industry. And as the scale advances, so the costs would be expected to fall, in competition with incumbent fossil fuel industries that fossil fuels cannot and will not win. So, Forrest is thinking big – really big. And his initial investment announcements are not just for solar or wind farms – enormous as these are likely to be – but for critical components of new green hydrogen-based value chains, such as the manufacture and installation of electrolyzers, pipelines and cables.

FFI under Forrest is embarked on a major investment plunge into a green hydrogen future, announcing a series of investment initiatives in the final months of 2021.

- Creation of the first stage of a green hydrogen hub in Gladstone (QLD), involving the manufacture of electrolyzers for splitting water into hydrogen and oxygen, as well as manufacture of infrastructure items for green hydrogen like pipelines, cabling and refuelling stations;
- Construction of the world's largest 250 MW green hydrogen facility at Bell Bay (Tas), to come online after 2023;
- Creation of a hub for production of hydrogen-containing fuel, methane, for use in the production of fertilizers, on Gibson Island, Brisbane (QLD), converting the Incitec Pivot fertilizer plant to run on green hydrogen;
- Creation of a $1.3 billion hybrid gas and hydrogen plant at Port Kembla (NSW); and
- Creation of a thin film solar manufacturing plant, again in Brisbane, in partnership with Dutch green energy start-up HyET.

These are indicators of the likely future scale of the solar-hydrogen economy. It is notable that these FFI initiatives are all based on manufacturing, and on ramping up the scale of the manufacturing processes and bringing down costs accordingly. Forrest's vision is that, when scaled up like this, the green hydrogen manufacturing processes will plunge in cost (due to learning curves) and will accordingly grow the scale of the market to challenge the grip of the incumbent fossil fuel industries. This is the global green shift in action.[25]

Another gigantic industrial initiative has been announced by Mukesh Ambani, founder and head of the Indian fossil fuels group, Reliance Industries Ltd, in which Ambani spells out industrial initiatives amounting to $75 billion involving green hydrogen – in a complete break with fossil fuels. This goal includes a target of producing 100 GW of renewable energy capacity, a fifth of India's target for non-fossil capacity by 2030.[26] Ambani is on record as vowing to produce the green hydrogen from water at a cost below $1 per kg – or a 60 per cent reduction in current costs.

The advantage in utilizing these existing industrial hubs as sites for green hydrogen propagation is that they work with already established interconnected value chains and provide local employment which can be readily redeployed in new green hydrogen garb. Such redeployment provides insurance against unemployment for workers already employed in fossil fuel activities, thereby removing one of the principal barriers to uptake of the green hydrogen economy.

These then are some of the pathways through which green hydrogen is transforming and decarbonizing industrial processes. All are indications of industrial possibilities for carbon reduction across several pathways, where the technical feasibility awaits only the essential scaling-up to drive down costs and thereby raise market share. This is actually a well-established perspective in economics – but one that has been comprehensively ignored in standard textbook presentations. Climate change discussions continue to focus on a comparative static framework, namely how prices might be adjusted via carbon taxes or emissions trading. Useful as these policies might be in making life more difficult for fossil fuels, they have not demonstrated the potential to drive a total hydrogen industrial revolution.

For that, we need to broaden our perspective and enrol economic thinking that has been largely ignored in climate discussions so far. We turn to investigate these possibilities in the next chapter.

---

25 See my earlier works Mathews (2015; 2017; 2019) for an exposition of this argument.
26 See 'The $75 billion to make India a Hydrogen Hub', *The Japan Times*, 30 January 2022, at: The $75 billion plan to make India a hydrogen hub | The Japan Times.

Chapter 4

A GREEN GROWTH ECONOMY

Division of labour depends upon the extent of the market, but the extent of the market also depends upon the division of labour. In this circumstance lies the possibility of economic progress which comes as the result of the new knowledge which men [humankind] are able to gain.

—Allyn Young 1928

In the lead up to the 26th Conference of the Parties (COP 26) under the UN Framework Convention on Climate Change (UNFCCC), held in Glasgow in November 2021, all attention was focused on individual country commitments to carbon reductions (Intended Nationally Determined Contributions, INDCs), in the hope that in aggregate this would lead to substantial global reductions. But it has to be said that this will not happen and will never happen for as long as commitments continue to be made within the worn-out conventions of the Kyoto Agreement (1997–2016) and its successor the Paris Agreement (2015–2021 and beyond). These agreements were framed solely in terms of low-carbon outcomes and aspirational commitments to reach such outcomes by individual countries, and never in terms of how the world can actually reach such outcomes through the greening of industrial processes (i.e. through a green industrial revolution) and complementary greening of finance.[1] There were no commitments in the Kyoto Protocol to promote solar or wind power industries, nor green hydrogen, nor any means to favour these industries in world trading agreements. It is long overdue that such a shift in perspective should inform international agreements on the mitigation of climate change.

To focus solely on outcomes as done in the Kyoto and Paris agreements is consistent with conventional economics reasoning couched in terms of

---

1 It's also worth pointing out that commitments to deal with carbon emissions by national governments ignore the point that most emissions emanate from processes conducted by global corporations that can evade national control. This is another reason for seeking a solution in terms of a global successor to fossil fuels in the form of green hydrogen.

comparative static shifts from one product or process to another, driven by changes in price secured through the tax system. In this comparative static framework, we have carbon taxes (and their international extension in terms of border carbon tariffs) levied on economic processes to 'restore' an equilibrium between carbon-intensive processes (using incumbent fossil fuels both as energy vectors and as petrochemical inputs) and new 'carbon-light' processes that substitute renewables for fossil fuels. Something deeper is needed to capture the real dynamics of the green transition.

The whole debate over carbon taxes has proceeded over the past couple of decades without the benefit of empirical evidence as to whether or not carbon taxes actually work. They are advocated on the basis of typical a priori reasoning that afflicts all of conventional neoclassical economics. This reasoning has carried over to debates over what to do about global warming, held under the aegis of the UNFCCC – with the Glasgow COP 26 as the latest instalment in this process. Comparative static reasoning has its place, but it should be a complement to dynamic thinking involving industrial transformation and evolution. But conventional neoclassical thinking is fixated on the comparative static to the almost total neglect of the dynamic.[2] It is self-evident that the green transition – involving such substitutions as wind and solar power for coal-fired power, battery-powered electric vehicles (BEVs) and fuel cell-powered electric vehicles (FCEVs) for internal combustion engines, and green hydrogen for natural gas – must depend not just on these individual substitutions but on systemic transformations involving the emergence of a new 'green' industrial system from the matrix of the incumbent fossil fuel system.[3] Nothing else could sustain such a comprehensive transformation.

The last occasions on which such systemic (technoindustrial) transitions took place were in the early twentieth century when mass production took over from prior craft-based systems, and subsequent transformations within mass production such as 'just-in-time production' as invented in Japan and

---

2 Consider the case of the economist William Nordhaus, winner of the 2018 'Nobel' prize in economics, whose latest book (2021), *The Spirit of Green*, lays out a view of economics as rectifying externalities across the board, not just in climate change discussions. For a discussion of Nordhaus' work and (comparative static) climate models, see 'Check your spillover: The Climate Colossus' by Geoff Mann, *London Review of Books*, 44 (3) (10 February 2022), at: Geoff Mann Check Your Spillover: The Climate Colossus LRB 10 February 2022.

3 Major initiatives in Korean FCEVs, involving the national government working closely with companies such as Hyundai, are described in one of the case studies carried in the forthcoming book *Developmental Environmentalism* (Thurbon, Kim, Tan and Mathews (2023)).

'total quality management' again invented in Japan. Nobody has ever argued (to my knowledge) that mass production of Ford automobiles in the United States was stimulated by a tax on horse and buggies, or that mass production of typewriters even earlier was stimulated by a tax on quill pens. Of course not. These were systemic transformations that were driven by their own principles sui generis, which turned on the capacity of entrepreneurs to envisage large-scale markets and invest in the large-scale production systems needed to create mass-produced standardized products for these new markets. The notion that a tax on carbon could stimulate and drive a post-fossil fuels industrial revolution likewise strains credulity.

In the mass production system, the standardized product and process innovations involved were what gave the system its capacity to reap huge economies of scale and thereby undercut the preceding craft-based production systems on cost grounds. The lower costs emerged as a result of successive rounds of market expansion and cost reduction linked to manufacturing learning curves, leading to substantial profits. Traditional comparative static economic analysis based on static concepts of supply and demand, linked to static concepts like oligopoly and monopoly compared with 'perfect competition' (where all producers are the same), was quite unable to shed any light on the rise of this new system of standardized manufacture and on the new principles of its operation.

It was left to the US maverick economist Allyn Young to demonstrate the key principles of the new system in terms of how the innovative mass producers were able to capture increasing returns (as opposed to the diminishing returns that rule in agriculture and extractive industries) and through this to drive economic progress. His 1928 presidential address to the British Association for Advancement of Science (BAAS), 'Increasing returns and economic progress', carried subsequently in *The Economic Journal*, remains the single best outline of how mass production works and how it differs from the craft-based production that preceded it. Of course, it goes without saying that Young was comprehensively ignored by his economics peers, and he remains today as a marginal figure, a heterodox exponent of a heterodox economics.

From Marginal Incentives to Systemic Transformation

The times today call for heterodox economic reasoning, because the world is in the grip of another fundamental systemic transformation of the industrial system, this time from black to green energy. What we are witnessing is the evolution of the twentieth-century industrial system with energy based on fossil fuels to a twenty-first century industrial system based on circular processes and renewable energy resources and green hydrogen. It would be a forlorn hope to imagine that such a systemic transformation could be driven by static policy tools like carbon taxes or emissions trading schemes targeted at single substitutions. Such tools that operate at the margin may play a subsidiary role, but only as comparative static complements and supplements to fundamental Schumpeterian dynamic strategies aimed at the systemic core of the transformation.

This systemic core consists of fresh investments in new 'green' processes and their ousting of incumbent fossil fuel-based processes, in what Schumpeter (1942) described so memorably as 'creative destruction' – the creation of the new green industries based on investments in renewables and green hydrogen and the destruction of the incumbent fossil fuel industries. It is based on sound economic reasoning that entrepreneurs introducing the new can capture advantages based on lower costs and higher productivity as they oust the old.

As Allyn Young clearly explained, in his address to the BAAS in 1928, what drives investment in new industries is not so much the extent of the market for their produce, as the extent of the *potential market*, given that costs can be reduced – and thereby prices – because of the increase in the scale of production anticipated for a standardized product utilizing standardized processes. This is what actually drives cost reduction in mass production industries – and so, by a similar argument, what drives cost reduction in new green industries. The cost reduction, and the market expansion associated with it, is what drives the success of green products and processes as they oust products and processes based on fossil fuels. What investments do is radically shift the costs and the associated extent of the market, in a circular and cumulative fashion. The *flywheel of green investment* is an apt metaphor for the process – as utilized by 'Twiggy' Forrest and his company Fortescue Future Industries (FFI).[4]

As discussed in the preceding chapter, Forrest's FFI has colossal targets that guide its present investments. The company is on record as aiming for the production of 15 million tonnes of green hydrogen per annum by

---

4 Twiggy Forrest introduced the 'Flywheel of green industry' in his ABC Boyer Lecture (February 2021) with these words. 'At Fortescue, we call this the flywheel. We nudge the wheel, make sure our systems work, reduce costs, free up capital and create demand. Then we encourage with that momentum to reduce costs even further, creating an even larger, more reliable supply, that again creates more demand. The flywheel begins to spin on its own, faster and faster. Now, we're building, at global scale, the flywheel of green energy'. See Oil vs Water: Confessions of a carbon emitter), ABC Boyer Lecture, at: 01 | Oil vs Water — Confessions of a carbon emitter - Boyer Lectures - ABC Radio National.

2030 and 50 million tonnes per annum by 2050.[5] These amounts call for correspondingly huge wind farms and solar farms to generate the required green electricity at scale in the regions adjacent to the green hydrogen production plants – of the order of an onshore wind farm of capacity 1,683 GW or an offshore wind farm of capacity 1,331 GW (1.3 TW).[6] The largest wind and solar farm announced so far for Australia's northern regions is the 26 GW hybrid solar-wind Asian Renewable Energy Hub. So more than 65 such hubs would be needed to produce FFI's target for green hydrogen of 15 million tonnes per year by 2030. A daunting target indeed – but one that is not beyond the scale of practicability.

The announced investments by FFI are strategic, in the sense that they set the stage for other investments to follow in their wake in a process best described as circular and cumulative causation (C&CC). In Gladstone (Qld), FFI plans to invest in manufacturing facilities for electrolyzers which will be the principal piece of equipment needed for producing green hydrogen by splitting it from water using renewable electric power. With this $1 billion-plus investment announcement, FFI creates both the essential means for producing green hydrogen at colossal scale (and at a cost lower than the $1.2 million per MW that currently prevails in Europe) and the demand for renewable power at a greater scale than previously envisaged, boosting solar and wind power generation in and near the Gladstone Basin which has previously been the coal capital of Queensland.

Likewise the Indian industrialist Mukesh Ambani has announced major green hydrogen investment proposals amounting to $75 billion – taking his fossil fuels firm Reliance Industries in a completely new post-fossil fuels direction. As if channelling Allyn Young, Ambani sets an ambitious target for his proposed green hydrogen investments, anticipating not the present size of the hydrogen market (still quite small) but its anticipated size as the solar-hydrogen economy propagates itself.

5　See Forrest's speech to the Clean Energy Council Summit, 18 August 2021, at: Dr Andrew Forrest AO delivers speech at Clean Energy Council summit | Fortescue Future Industries (ffi.com.au).

6　Now 1 kg hydrogen contains 120-142 MJ (megajoules) of energy. Using Platt's formula, 1 TWh of green electricity is needed to produce 20,000 tonnes of green hydrogen. So 15 million tonnes green hydrogen per year would call for 5,017 to 5,937 TWh of green electricity each year, generated by (say) 1,331 GW (1.3 TW) of offshore wind (CF 43 per cent) or 1,683 GW (1.7 TW) of onshore wind (CF 34 per cent). See 'A wake-up call on green hydrogen: The amount of wind and solar needed is immense', by Leigh Collins, *Recharge*, 19/20 March 2020, at: A wake-up call on green hydrogen: the amount of wind and solar needed is immense | Recharge (rechargenews.com).

Forrest is capturing in his metaphor of the flywheel the notion that business works through repeated connections and processes of cost reduction (which means generating increasing returns) in a way that mimics the growing momentum of the flywheel as it spins. Another metaphor for the same process is that of the 'chain reaction' (Kaldor, 1970) which likewise captures the way that the growth of new industries proceeds through making multiple connections that propagate through the economy, like new shoots in a growing biosystem, like a grove of bamboo.[7]

Green Growth Economics

Green hydrogen is critical to the emergent green economy because it provides a buffer that enables renewable energy generation to proceed smoothly, while at the same time facilitating the production of the principal material flows through the industrial economy – green steel, green cement, green glass and so on. The irreducibly varying nature of solar and wind power (known therefore as varying renewable sources) is a major hurdle when compared with the commodity basis of fossil fuels – but it can be compensated (corrected) with suitable buffers such as batteries (to store energy in chemical form) or green hydrogen, which acts as both a store and carrier of energy.[8] Forrest and FFI are already thinking of green hydrogen as a replacement for oil and natural gas in their entirety. Forrest is on the public record as envisaging the scale of the green hydrogen economy reaching $12 trillion by 2050 – making it by far the largest industry on the planet. This is the scale of thinking on the part of an entrepreneur who aims not just to substitute one product or process for another but to replace entire industries.

The question of increasing returns is critical to the green revolution, because it is the possibility of securing the green growth that is needed for green economic progress. Green growth must be distinguished from the black or brown growth associated with greater levels of dirty resource throughput in the incumbent economy. There is a well-known school of thought (associated with Herman Daly and followers) which states that economic growth cannot continue forever on a finite planet.[9] And if by growth is meant growth in GDP, meaning growing output created by growing inputs, then Daly et al

---

7 It is worth noting that the term for green shoots of bamboo, Hsinchu (Xinju), was adopted in Taiwan for the nation's high-tech development hub.

8 Note that green hydrogen acts as a store and carrier of energy; the energy has to be produced from solar sources like renewable energy devices.

9 See for example Daly (1974). For a well-known text in the Daly tradition, see Jackson (2009).

are certainly correct. You cannot squeeze extensive growth forever from a finite material base.

But Allyn Young reminds us (1928) that growth can more fundamentally mean *intensive* growth, viz growth in output from a constant or declining resource base. Intensive growth is based on increasing returns, where lower costs and improved productivity drive market expansion which when repeated successively (circular and cumulative causation (CCC)) generates economic growth in the absence of growth in resource inputs – or 'green growth'.[10]

Growth that is measured in increases in GDP is usually *extensive* growth, associated with increasing flows of materials and energy through the economic system. This clearly cannot continue indefinitely – and which indeed must be curbed as a matter of the highest urgency. But *intensive growth* is a different matter entirely. This refers to growth in value without change in the underlying flow of resources, through increasing levels of recirculation and greater degrees of inter-firm exchange intensity. Individual firms, and value chains of firms, will doubtless continue to seek out opportunities to generate increasing returns – just as all capitalist firms before them have done. But increasing returns have (until recently) been ignored in mainstream economic analysis.

Increasing returns were banished from economic analysis for reasons solely to do with mathematical tractability of the equations governing supply and demand at equilibrium (no convergence to equilibrium can be demonstrated where increasing returns apply). But in capitalist reality, as opposed to the neoclassical fictions that purport to describe it, the search for increasing returns governs strategy. In totality, it is increasing returns that create the possibilities for intensive growth. The firms earning increasing returns (on which their profits rest) propagate via inter-firm connections through the process of CCC as described by Kaldor, Myrdal and others. These ideas, which have languished at the margins of economics for so long, should come into their own now as the debate between intensive and extensive growth becomes sharper in light of its significance for mitigating climate change.

A perspective on the green industrial revolution informed by the insights of Allyn Young, Nicholas Kaldor or Gunnar Myrdal enables us to register that what we are witnessing today is a comprehensive transformation of economic value chains with all their inter-linkages and opportunities for generating

---

10 It all depends, of course, on how one defines 'growth'. It is the difference between *intensive* and *extensive* growth that is fundamental – a point made by Jones (1988) in his discussion of economic growth, namely: 'To make sense of the strands of history, it is vital to distinguish between industrialization, capitalism, modern economic growth, *intensive* and *extensive* growth, and economic development'. Eric Jones, *Growth Recurring*, 1988.

increasing returns. The switch is from value chains based on fossil fuels (as inputs and as energy sources) to alternatives based on renewable and circular resource flows, where entrepreneurs create new value chains based on capturing increasing returns and thereby fashioning an economy based on green intensive growth. The strategies that deliver this outcome are those based on Schumpeterian insights, involving fresh investments that drive creative destruction, rather than strategies based on restoration of a putative equilibrium, such as carbon taxes and border carbon adjustments.

Putting green hydrogen at the centre of this transformation makes sense, because green hydrogen acts simultaneously as the new dominant fuel for transport, as the new source for energy storage and as a new source of industrial heat in green steel or green cement production. Each of these uses calls for green hydrogen to act as input into some processes and calls for fresh infrastructure. Increasingly the green hydrogen will be sourced from water via manufactured devices and processes that will come to resemble photosynthesis – that is artificial photosynthesis and photocatalysis. The green hydrogen economy will emerge as new value chains propagated based on hydrogen as common input.

The various green hydrogen-based value chains can be expected to link up with one another just like the stones on the GO game board, where the idea is to build interconnected patterns in competition with an opponent. It is cross-linkages between new hydrogen-based value chains that propagate through the incumbent fossil fuel economy to create a new renewable-based, green economy. (See Figure 2 for a typical sequence of moves in GO highlighting the sequential interconnections between stones on the board.) One value chain terminating in the production of electrolyzers might intersect with a value chain leading to the production of green hydrogen while another might intersect with green ammonia produced from green hydrogen and terminating in the production of green fertilizer. Entrepreneurs make strategic investments in these fresh value chains, looking to build competitive advantages as they capture the cost advantages of new green technology – such as new green steel forged by introducing green hydrogen in place of carbon for steel, or new green cement produced with green hydrogen as input in place of carbon-based inputs. The more value chains created in this way, with their multiple interactions, the stronger are the green industrial clusters they generate.

Intensive vs. Extensive Growth

Green growth is a smart term because it appears to be a contradiction: how can an economy both grow and be green? Surely greenness and growth contradict each other. But it is a contradiction only when growth is viewed as

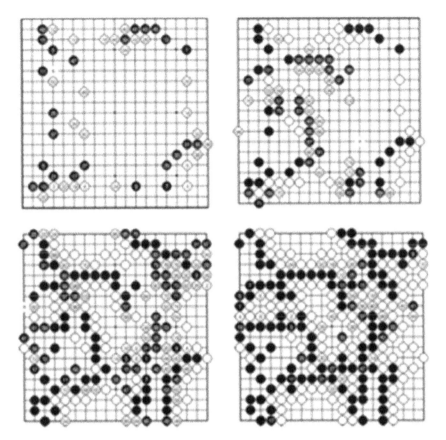

Figure 2 Sequence of additions in the game of GO. Adapted from Mathews (2011).

extensive growth – as growth in the economy's resource base, or as growth in the scale of physical production, with expanded inputs of resources and expanded physical output. But growth is equally susceptible to an alternative definition as growth in economic performance – involving incomes and wealth. If the economy is decoupled from its physical and energy basis, then it can grow without expansion in its physical character. This is what is described as *intensive growth* – and I argue that it is essential to make this distinction if the debate over green growth strategies is to make any progress and if the case for the solar-hydrogen economy is to become mainstream.[11]

---

11 See my 2011 *Futures* paper for a discussion. Unfortunately the OECD report *Towards Green Growth* makes no such distinction between extensive and intensive economic growth. It refers to growth that is capital-intensive, or energy-intensive or carbon-intensive – but not growth that is intensive as opposed to extensive.

Intensive growth is the product of economic processes of interaction that draw on cluster effects, inter-organizational dynamics and industrial districts, resulting in what economists have long termed 'increasing returns' – as discussed above. It is helpful in understanding increasing returns to see them arising from synergistic effects that make the whole greater than the sum of its parts. If the output is represented as a production function, where output Y is depicted as a function of inputs including capital, labour as well as physical resources (generalized usually as land), then the increase in output resulting from an increase in inputs is represented by a growth equation. By contrast, the existence of intensive growth would be represented by an inequality, where the increase in output would exceed the immediate effect of the increase in inputs. It is clear that in probing these processes we are getting to the very core of what makes an economy function, and in particular why the green growth economy based on solar energy and hydrogen can be expected to become the dominant way of viewing economic progress.

It is concepts like increasing returns, clusters and systemic interactions that characterize the real progress achieved along green growth lines by emerging industrial giants like China and India. Increasing returns are generated (and so intensive green growth is accomplished) through the expansion of the green growth sector of the economy. This can be envisaged as groups of firms making interconnections in the same way that pieces strengthen each other in the ancient board game *Go*. This remains a vivid illustration of the expansion of the green growth economy within the matrix of the old fossil fuel and linear economy, which underpinned the rise of fossil fuels.

Green growth is articulated in this text as a sound normative goal for rapidly industrializing countries like China or India, and as providing the prescriptive setting within which policies like expanding the reach of renewable power grids make abundant sense. No one invented the green growth strategy in itself. There was some discussion of 'eco-development' in the 1970s and 1980s, but this petered out in the West. China has stumbled upon the notion while seeking to allay problems of immediate environmental pollution and energy security issues as well as resource security issues. It was a pragmatic turn on the part of the Chinese leadership. But once the benefits of the green growth strategy started to manifest themselves, the Chinese state (at central and provincial levels) was able to intervene in the economy to restructure it along green growth lines, utilizing green finance as the means to drive investment along new pathways.[12] This strategy has turned

---

12 See Lee (2021) for a recent discussion of China's state-led development strategies.

out to be a powerful means of reshaping an economy – far more powerful than the carbon taxes and cap and trade schemes so much discussed by neoclassical economists.

Meanwhile the traditional economic establishment puts up 'heroic' resistance to the green growth challenge. Some argue that 'green growth' is a contradiction in terms and that growth always means growth in resources and energy consumption that is incompatible with a finite world. This would be a deadly objection – if it were true. But there can be growth in incomes without growth in energy and resource throughput – as is the case with increasing returns. Indeed, this is the real meaning of the notion that there is an economic output produced by economic inputs that generate increasing returns. This is what industrializing countries like China are moving towards as they implement determined green energy and green resources (circular economy) strategies. While some argue that greening growth can create new jobs, mainstream economists insist in response that green policies can have an impact on the composition of investment and employment, but not on their absolute levels (e.g. Schmalensee, 2012). This is an assertion not supported by any evidence.

The case of China clearly demonstrates the contrary, namely that green investment can create jobs in great numbers – while the same state-led policy is reducing employment in fossil fuel industries, particularly coal. These are market-mediated policies being implemented in China – but they do not seem to be recognized as such by mainstream economists.[13] Other scholars like Antal and Van den Bergh (2014) view a Green Growth strategy as being impossibly difficult (based largely on vested interests reasoning) and fall back on zero growth – without considering the fatal impact that this would have on prospects for countries like China and India.

Meanwhile, mainstream economists continue to cast doubt on green growth initiatives in developing countries. We find economists like Collier and Venables (2012) arguing that green strategies in Africa go against

---

13 The mainstream economist Schmalensee (2012) queries both demand-side and supply-side policies for stimulating green growth in the United States, insisting that they have had perverse outcomes. 'Particularly in recent years, the state requirements have been explicitly intended to create in-state employment. The result of all this has been remarkable growth in both wind and solar electric generation, which has served to increase the cost of electricity – some of which is borne by taxpayers, not ratepayers' [2012: S4]. Compare this with the case in China, where state guidance through the Five Year Plans channels investment towards solar and wind device manufacturing as well as solar and wind power generation. As the market expands so the costs decline, through the effect of the learning curve.

the comparative advantages that African countries are supposed to have in traditional non-green industries. Schmalensee himself argues that 'Africa's shortages of capital, skills, and regulatory capacity make green options relatively expensive, while its natural endowments of fossil fuels make their uses relatively cheap' (2012: S5). These arguments have not stood the test of time, as solar power becomes cheaper to generate than burning fossil fuels. Indeed, the argument is tantamount to proposing that all that the poor need is fossil fuels; or that provision of fossil fuels fulfils a moral obligation on the part of the rich world to the poor world. A closer look at the same situation reveals that African countries have everything to gain by moving to build their economies around green energy and resource flows. African countries can leapfrog their competitors in Western countries by moving swiftly to adopt solar and wind power to feed a green hydrogen industry while reducing their (sometimes onerous) costs of importing fossil fuels.[14]

By contrast, green growth promises to provide guidance for realistic and feasible industrialization strategies pursued by emerging giants like China and India and to be emulated by emerging economies in Africa, Asia and elsewhere. Green growth is more focused and explicit than the vague goal of 'sustainable development', while being sharply different from the current Western favourites of 'zero growth' and even degrowth. In this chapter I have argued that green growth implies an alternative view of how the economy works, focused more on clusters and industrial districts than on individual firms; on growth as an intensive phenomenon driven by market expansion; and on manufacturing as the source of increasing returns.

A Sixth Techno-Economic Paradigm Shift

A final issue to deal with is the perspective on the emergence of the green hydrogen economy as a novel techno-economic paradigm, viewed within a neo-Schumpeterian setting of successive techno-economic surges. There is by now widespread scholarly agreement on the framework of successive techno-economic surges, which began with the pioneering work of Freeman and Perez, and has been continued by Carlota Perez working on her own

---

14 See 'African path to avoid fossil fuel dependency', by Andrew Ward, *Financial Times*, 10 November 2016, at: https://www.ft.com/content/c168de08-9f8f-11e6-891e-abe238dee8e2.

or with collaborators.[15] As outlined by Perez, there are five such surges that started with the traditional industrial revolution, encompassing (1) mechanization, factories and coal power (from 1771); (2) steam and railways (from 1829); (3) steel, electricity and heavy engineering (from 1875); (4) mass production, automobiles and oil (from 1908); and (5) infotech (from 1971). The basic concept that underpins the work of Freeman and Perez is that a new cluster of technologies is introduced with wide-ranging effects, based on the fact that the cost of the major input is below that of incumbent technology, its cost is falling, and as a general-purpose technology it has multiple effects. This is a powerful framework that is backed by much historical research; it makes sense of the historically validated technological surges, placing them in a finance and state involvement setting that matches reality.

Is there a sixth such techno-economic paradigm, coming at a gap of around a half-century from the emergence of the fifth techno-economic surge that was precipitated in the 1970s by the advent of the computer and microprocessor? I myself answered this question in the affirmative, in a paper published in the journal *Futures* in 2013. In this paper, I argued that renewable energies constituted such a new paradigm that satisfied the conditions governing diffusion of the new as outlined by Perez, namely that the new technology should be low cost, with a cost that is falling, and which has multiple applications as a general-purpose technology. But I was premature in making this assessment. While I saw renewables as having multiple applications, I did not consider the range of industrial processes that could be potentially transformed by a new energy source.

It is in fact the solar-hydrogen economy that fulfils the conditions for the emergence and diffusion of a new techno-economic paradigm surge. As emphasized in this text, a solar-hydrogen economy can be seen as having costs of production and distribution of green hydrogen as lower than the costs of fossil fuels (with all their geopolitical complications), and as having costs which are falling, because of the effect of the learning (experience) curve associated with manufacturing. In this case, the green hydrogen economy as energy source may definitely be viewed as a general-purpose technology, as a new energy source transforming multiple industrial sectors as well as transport sectors (heavy trucks, rail, shipping and air), power generation and

---

15 For a synoptic view of the literature on technological surges and their drivers, see Perez and Murray-Leach (2021) as well as Perez (2016). Debates on the green transition within the innovations literature have been engaged in by, e.g. Schot and Steinmueller (2018) and Fagerberg (2022). For my own contribution to this techno-economic surge literature and the role of green energy, see Mathews (2013) as well as subsequent contributions in my 2015 and 2017 books.

domestic sectors. It is the very universality of the substitution effect of green hydrogen, in ousting incumbent fossil fuel technologies, that makes it a candidate for the sixth techno-economic surge transforming the global industry. Such a perspective underlines the insurgency of the green hydrogen transition and its links with past techno-economic surges and their dramatic social impacts.[16] Here is a rich field of scholarship to be investigated further by scholars working in a neo-Schumpeterian tradition.

---

16 This perspective on a sixth techno-economic paradigm (TEP) shift is at variance with the popular view that industry is currently being transformed by a fourth industrial revolution, spanning artificial intelligence, robotics and the internet of things, counting as previous industrial revolutions the computer, the internal combustion engine and the steam engine. The term Industry 4.0 was introduced by Klaus Schwab in 2015 at the World Economic Forum.

Chapter 5

PERSPECTIVES FROM THE FUTURE: TWILIGHT OF FOSSIL FUELS

I opened my 2015 book *Greening of Capitalism* with the argument that industrial capitalism had created a world of wealth that was as unexpected as it was unlikely. Manufacturing industry liberated the countries of the West from age-old Malthusian constraints and had created the Great Divergence between the Western world and the impoverished 'Rest'. But after the countries of East Asia (led by Japan) closed the gap in the twentieth century, using state-led catch-up strategies, and the twenty-first century saw the turn of the 'sleeping giants' like China and India likewise rising to claim their place in the sun, the question of what kind of industrialization might be on offer came to prominence.

My argument (which strikes me as valid now as it was then) is that a model of industrialization based on fossil fuels usage and unlimited resource plundering would not work, because it would not scale. What was becoming difficult for the countries that had actually pioneered an industrial revolution would be quite impossible for countries like China and India as they attempted to follow suit and lift their vast populations out of poverty. They were confronting the necessity of adopting a 'green growth' model of industrial capitalism founded on renewable energy (based on manufacturing) and a circular economy – because green growth would be the only pathway to industrialization that could scale to the level needed by these national giants without destroying the earth.

The evidence has only grown stronger that this is indeed the path being followed by China and India, and followers like Brazil or Vietnam, as an alternative to a strategy based on the lottery of allocations of fossil fuels and resource commodities. The rise of China gives the appearance of inevitability as it appropriates more and more of the global value added by manufacturing, and of GDP generally, as shown in Figure 3. Non-OECD countries (for which, read China) appropriated more of the world economy than OECD countries by 2010 and have maintained the gap ever since.

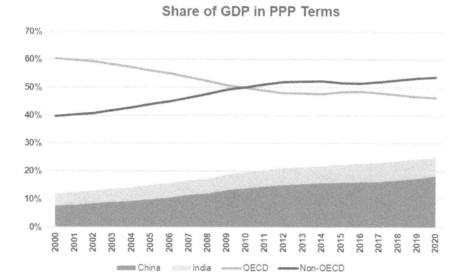

Figure 3 Share of Global GDP: OECD vs non-OECD. *Source:* Author's calculation based on data of the World Bank (https://data.worldbank.org/).

As China (and eventually India) become world leaders in manufacturing, so they will face the necessity of making hard choices over energy. I have been pursuing an argument for several years now that China (and eventually India) would become a leader in green technologies (renewables, batteries, electric vehicles and electrolyzers), driven by geopolitical necessity and energy/resource security rather than by any aspirations to mitigate climate change. This argument is sound and has only been strengthened by the evidence in intervening years. Chart 4 shows how China has continued to green its electric power system with a proportion of power capacity generated by water (hydro), wind and sun (WWS) that continues to rise. Figure 4 shows that in China the renewables – solar, wind and hydro – have been accounting for a rising proportion of electricity generated (and for generating capacity). China has raised its WWS-installed capacity from 20 per cent to 43 per cent – a 23 per cent increase in 15 years, or 1.5 per cent increase in green electric capacity each year. This is a conscious choice on the part of China, and – once linked to green hydrogen – paves the way to a consistent introduction of a solar-hydrogen economy.

I framed this argument a few years ago to help explain why China (and to some extent India) was emerging as a green industries leader. So how does this argument fare in light of the evidence on the solar-hydrogen economy (which postdates my two books published in 2015 and 2017)? At this stage, there is no obvious leadership on the part of China (apart from the 2025 goal of 200,000 tonnes green hydrogen), nor in India apart from the (very important)

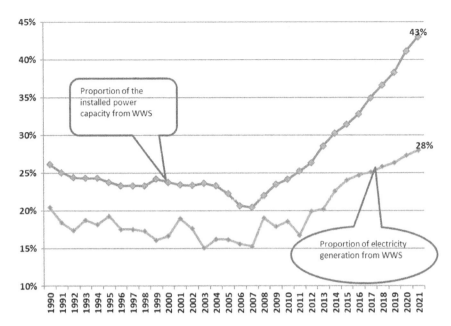

Figure 4 Greening of China's electric power system, 1990 to 2021. *Source:* Author's calculation based on CEC and NBS China.

initiative announced by Reliance Industries head Mukesh Ambani. It may be that the Chinese and Indian states are waiting to see how fast costs (and prices) decline in the technologies of the solar-hydrogen economy and that they will elect to enter as fast followers once they judge the time to be ripe.

In the meantime, the world of the solar-hydrogen economy is very much a world of advanced countries investing in advanced technologies in advanced ways, using their full technological and financial capacities to do so. But unlike China, in the West the fossil fuel companies continue to exercise an outsize influence over energy policy, making the transition to a green hydrogen economy a fraught affair.

The first two decades of the twenty-first century have witnessed an emerging but fierce political debate over energy strategy that has sharpened as the prognosis over global warming becomes more pressing. While the scientific consensus and the successive reports of the IPCC and UNFCC point to the inevitability of a transition away from fossil fuels, the political dominance of coal-, oil- and gas-interests continues to fragment any consensus over the needed energy transition.

The politics of energy in the twentieth century have moved from being 100 per cent focused on promoting fossil fuels and ensuring their secure delivery to a politics in the twenty-first century where the dominance of fossil fuels is contested and the alternative in the form of the solar-hydrogen economy comes to be seen as realistic and practical.[1] The rise of renewables as low-cost energy and sustainable energy sources has been the curtain raiser for this emerging political drama, as fossil fuels vs the solar-hydrogen economy comes to occupy centre-stage in the struggle over the future of our industrial civilization and its energy drivers.

From the perspective of 2050, when the solar-hydrogen economy should be well advanced, the present dominance of fossil fuels may seem to resemble a wild aberration. Why would a civilization mortgage its future to the vagaries of randomly allocated fossil fuels with all their geopolitical complications, their environmental disasters, their endlessly fluctuating prices and their peaking supplies? By contrast, the solar-hydrogen energy system offers democratic access for all because of its foundations in manufacturing (and hence a reduction in global tensions); the relative safety and security of solar and electrical systems as compared with the lottery of fossil fuel resources; and the certainty of reducing costs and the security of sustainable circular energy-industrial processes that endlessly recycle materials and energy. Assuming our industrial civilization does indeed survive the looming global warming catastrophe and successfully transitions to a solar-hydrogen future, our children and their children will marvel at how we managed to expose ourselves to such absurdly high risks and play dice with their future.

The solar-hydrogen economy can be expected to teach us humility. As opposed to its mischaracterization as a strategy fit only for the wealthy countries, it promises to generate economic growth and prosperity, while teaching us to live within our solar income. These are entirely favourable prospects, for developed as much as for developing countries.

Issues Involved in the Green Hydrogen Transition

Whatever the favourable prospects for the solar-hydrogen economy, and whatever might be the obstacles thrown up by fossil fuel interests and their haphazard energy choices, there are issues involved in the transition to hydrogen that genuinely call for debate. One of these is the relationship between electrification and resort to hydrogen as a general-purpose fuel. Apart from the debate between battery-powered electric vehicles and fuel cell-powered electric vehicles, crystallized in Elon Musk's famous comment that fuel cells are 'a mind-bogglingly stupid technology' (discussed above), there is a real

---

1 For a comprehensive survey of these contested energy debates of the twenty-first century, see Thompson (2021; 2022).

issue that as electrification and battery energy storage improve and expand, the scope (and necessity) for hydrogen – green or otherwise – can be expected to contract. Is the relationship between electrification and hydrogen really zero-sum?[2]

It may be anticipated that electrification of transport will continue to improve or expand. In shipping there are already battery-powered ferries in Scandinavian waters, while there are electric (battery-powered) trucks and buses in heavy road transport. These provide a competitive alternative not just to gasoline or diesel-powered engines, but to hydrogen-powered fuel cells. This will be healthy competition, driving innovation in both options that are alternatives to fossil fuels.

In heavy industries like steel, cement and glass, there really is no competition between hydrogen and electrification – the two go hand in hand, as complements. In steel for example electric arc furnaces can expand while hydrogen as a reducing input can also expand. Electrification and use of hydrogen are complementary in the strong sense that in combination they reduce the scope for fossil fuels, in a process where each step makes the next step easier – a process best described as circular and cumulative causation. But electrification and use of hydrogen are also competitive options where the competition promises to be healthy, promoting innovation and energy efficiency.

But competition with fossil fuels does not portend anything so favourable. It is the deliberate obstruction by fossil fuel and nuclear interests of the green hydrogen transition that looms as the main obstacle to a smooth transition to a solar-hydrogen economy. Oil companies stand in a critical position; they might elect to move with the transition, bringing their expertise in scale management to the hydrogen economy, or they might attempt to block the transition, seeking to prolong the life of their fossil fuel investments. The choice they make will be central to the emerging politics of the green (hydrogen) energy transition. And central to these choices will be the relative dominance of mainstream economic perspectives.

The Politics of Energy Transition

The political momentum behind the clean energy transition has been frustrated not just by the opposition of fossil fuels companies but by the endless

---

2 See the 2020 study by Volkswagen which comes down on the side of BEVs as compared with FCEVs, at: https://www.greencarreports.com/news/1127660_battery-electric-or -hydrogen-fuel-cell-vw-lays-out-why-one-is-the-winner.

dominance of the narrow economics perspective on raising prices for fossil fuels – carbon taxes and emissions trading schemes – and seeking to balance these raised prices/costs with continued employment in the energy industries. Raising prices as a purported means of driving consumption away from fossil fuels runs into immediate short- and medium-term problems. It is a wrong-headed perspective. What should inform the debate instead is a focus on the industries of the future, and on promoting their advantages through declining costs associated with renewables and green hydrogen and their promise of jobs for the future, as employment in the fossil fuels sector declines. Raising costs through taxes (i.e. carbon taxes) is a wrong-headed strategy; by contrast, reducing costs through a focus on the green hydrogen economy and technological learning curves to make the new solar-hydrogen sectors more competitive is a much more sensible survival strategy. The former is seen as a barrier; the latter as a facilitator.

Climate change has been met by a politics focused almost exclusively on carbon emissions reduction by whatever means seem feasible. The extreme case is that of intended nationally determined contributions framed by the Paris Agreement and which allow individual countries to volunteer future reductions in emissions without any reference to the technologies or industries that would be involved. Indeed when countries get serious about promoting policies to build their green industries, utilizing such trade instruments as Local Content Requirements (LCRs), they find themselves hauled before the tribunals of the World Trade Organization and threatened with being expelled from the world trade systems (with disastrous results for manufacturing and employment in the countries concerned). This is precisely what happened to India when it introduced its National Solar Mission that encompassed carefully crafted LCRs to promote a domestic solar PV industry in India – with clear negative impact on India's subsequent investments in its solar PV sector.[3]

A way around this impasse would be for the principal organizations involved in climate change and world trade and industry – the UNFCCC on the one hand and WTO on the other – to reach an agreement or Concordat in which climate change would be recognized as an overarching danger that would justify relaxing otherwise stringent restrictions on the capacity of countries to promote their own green industries. There could be a time limit imposed on such relaxations – for, say, 10 years. Such a Climate Concordat would signal an awareness that climate change can only be curbed once

---

3 See my paper on this issue in the journal *Climate Policy* (Mathews 2016).

countries approach its mitigation through industrial policies designed to promote green industries.

Here the green hydrogen economy would present itself as the logical end-
goal of such green industrial policies, moving the world (and the UNFCCC
and WTO) on from the debilitating concerns with comparative static policies
like raising carbon prices or emissions trading schemes and instead moving
towards policies designed to actively promote new, green industries, focused
on the generation, storage, distribution and utilization of green hydrogen
throughout the economy.

Such an alternative view would herald a politics based on the driving force
of industrial change, couched in terms of the rise of new energy industries and
the decline of the incumbents. It would be a politics based on Schumpeter's
clear-eyed view of *creative destruction* as the motor of change, with a sense of
the need to support and promote the new (renewables, green hydrogen and
circular economy) and reduce previous support for the incumbents (fossil fuels
in all their forms). Supporting investment in the new industries (green hydrogen and its associated activities) promotes employment, exports and industrial competitiveness. Propping up declining industries like coal or coal-fired
power or vehicles with internal combustion engines stands against the dominant trends of the time. It is not a recipe for sound politics.

Where alternative economic interests see their future in promoting clean
energy – as in Germany where the *Energiewende* rules or Japan – then the politics plays out differently. German renewable energy interests were responsible
for driving home the innovative form of financial support in the form of feed-
in tariffs (as masterminded by the late Hermann Scheer) while they provided
the rock-solid support for the anti-nuclear movement that was needed as the
passport to a clean and green energy system. As Scheer well understood, it
was the emergence of economic interests in renewables on the part of new
renewables-based companies that made the difference in the emergence of
the Greens as a powerful political force in Germany – and elsewhere.[4]

Meanwhile in the United States as a lingering desire to see American oil
independence fuelled the rise of the fracking revolution, so it destroyed any
possibility of the United States being able to lead a green industrial revolution. Even where fossil fuel interests dominate – as in Australia where coal and
gas exports have been world leaders – the breakthrough to a green industrial
revolution can occur, driven by far-sighted business interests. This is arguably
what is occurring with the switch in the 2020s by leading industrialists of
the fossil fuels era – such as Andrew 'Twiggy' Forrest of the Australian iron

---

4 See Scheer's work over many years, particularly Scheer (2011).

ore miner Fortescue Metals Group or the Indian magnate Mukesh Ambani, founder of the fossil fuels conglomerate Reliance Industries – as they swing behind strategies that break completely with the fossil fuels past.

Green hydrogen offers clear advantages for latecomer industrializing countries such as those in Africa which can build an industrial economy around alternatives to fossil fuels such as green hydrogen, thereby benefiting from the cost advantages (and declining costs) of hydrogen, as well as enhanced energy security in the form of manufactured energy and improved environmental conditions. Latecomer industrializers in Africa like Ethiopia can build advantages by creating their hydrogen economy ab initio while more advanced industrial economies are required to reset their industrial infrastructure. In either case it is the competitive dynamics triggered by innovation that drives the economy forward, as contrasted with the century of stagnation that characterized the fossil fuels era with its monopoly oil companies and monopoly auto giants – all relics of the past as the world moves to a hydrogen future.

It is the grand scale of the industrial vision shown by green industrialists that makes the difference – and sets the stage to create a completely new politics of the energy transition. Now the combination of the threat of climate change (global warming) and geopolitical hazard, with the availability of a comprehensive energy alternative to fossil fuels in the form of the solar-hydrogen economy, marks a new phase in energy debates. This time it is far-sighted industrialists who tend to be leading the way rather than states or political leaders. They are doing so for a combination of public responsibility and the quest for profits, in the sense that they comprehend the direction in which industry is evolving. I noted above how striking it is that in early 2022 there has been not a single political leader in the West who has grasped the full significance of the solar-hydrogen alternative and fashioned a political programme around its achievement.

Consider the US Green New Deal that seemed so promising when first developed and popularized, but now seems decidedly out of sync with moves to propel the solar-hydrogen economy. In its latest incarnation in the US Infrastructure Bill, in 2021, green hydrogen warrants scarcely a mention and is eclipsed by fossil fuels and natural gas-sourced hydrogen.[5]

So what is missing in the story of the solar-hydrogen economy – so far – is a credible politics of the transition informed by the full scale of the total substitution of one industrial system (based on fossil fuels and a linear economy) by another based on solar-hydrogen, renewables generally and a circular economy. Bold and imaginative industrialists have taken the lead and are

---

5 See Bipartisan Infrastructure Deal Hydrogen Plan Isn't Very Green – Bloomberg.

pointing the way to a comprehensively new system that marks a total break with fossil fuels. It is in fashioning such contrasts that politics should be playing a critical role. It is not just a matter of one or two more electrolyzers, or a few more electric vehicles, but a focus on the total transformation of the incumbent industrial system, with an emphasis on green steel, green cement, green fertilizers based on ammonia and other core industrial processes, that should be framing debate.

A century ago it was industrial entrepreneurs like Henry Ford who entertained such grand industrial visions, mastering investments in huge capacity increases that enabled them to capture greater markets as their costs declined. The same process is occurring today with industrial entrepreneurs investing in a green hydrogen future – like Andrew Forrest (Fortescue) in Australia or Mukesh Ambani (Reliance Industries) in India.

The politics of the transition to a solar-hydrogen economy promises to evolve into something quite different from the politics of oil or gas or coal. With fossil fuels the issues are the ownership of claims to the fossil resources and the protection of those claims; the financing of the infrastructural works such as pipelines; regulation of international trade and commerce, including management of the great markets like the NY Mercantile Exchange and the foreign exchange and futures trading in oil and gas; and in extreme cases the imposition of trade embargoes and blockades, such as the embargo imposed by the United States in the 1930s on Japan's imports of oil which led, more or less directly, to Japan's pre-emptive strike on Pearl Harbor in 1942 leading to the Pacific War.

In extreme cases the politics of oil becomes a matter of war – as experienced so often during the fossil fuels era with its endless succession of oil wars in the Middle East and elsewhere. Oil sanctions (as an extreme policy prescription) work because oil has become the central commodity needed by an industrial economy and because countries being sanctioned cannot 'manufacture' oil (although the Nazis tried very hard to do so in the Second World War). The threat of war stands as the central feature of the political economy of oil.

How different will be the politics of a solar-hydrogen economy. Here the emphasis promises to be on the manufacture of such elements of the hydrogen economy as hydrogen production systems (electrolyzers and their components) and hydrogen utilizing systems like fuel cells; hydrogen transport and distribution systems; the manufacture of hydrogen-powered vehicles, trains, buses, ships and eventually aircraft; and the manufacture of hydrogen-consuming steel, cement and ammonia systems. The emphasis will be on promoting trade and manufacture; the protection of intellectual property in these manufactured products; on the opening up of new trade routes (such as trading renewable power) and the forging of free trade agreements to promote trade in manufactured products and in renewable power; on the provision of employment and training in the new skills associated with electrolysis and manufacture of fuel cells; and the promotion of tax systems that are based on value added in manufacturing and not on the penalizing of labour.

Hydrogen does not lend itself to sanctions precisely because it can be manufactured via the operation of electrolyzers, where countries can make rational choices in their selection of policies and activities in embarking on manufacturing programmes. Manufacturing as the key to energy politics is on the side of peace, not war.

We are now at a turning point where the politics of the solar-hydrogen economy can be anticipated to overtake and succeed the outmoded politics of fossil fuels with their haphazard energy choices. Free trade in manufactured hydrogen, fuel cells and their components has the potential to overtake the cartels and protection arrangements that have accompanied oil and gas and coal, up to and including war. The politics of the green industrial revolution is about to confront and eventually overcome the extant politics of the fossil fuel system. It is a case where our industrial civilization 'grows up' and takes charge of its own energy future. We can only trust that this will happen in time.

What I have sought to convey in this short book is a sense of the drama of this confrontation – a struggle for the central character of our industrial civilization. The perspective that informs this book is that of 'total substitution' where the solar-hydrogen economy takes over and potentially displaces the incumbent fossil fuels economy with its haphazard energy choices – *in its entirety*. This is a drama of cosmic dimensions. It is the creation of a new giant of the world of energy. It is one that vastly exceeds the shift involving a few solar panels and wind turbines displacing coal-fired power stations, or battery electric vehicles displacing internal combustion engine powered vehicles – the sorts of substitutions envisaged by mainstream comparative static economic reasoning. It is rather a transition where one industrial system based on the miracle of fossil fuels, as means of powering and materially feeding an entire economy, is succeeded by another miracle, an economy based on sunlight, hydrogen and the global water cycle. Two miracles: one building wealth but spelling doom while the other is providing a clean and sustainable solution to the climate change conundrum. The acronym SHE judiciously captures how this hydrogen economy will be based on humility and prudence, two virtues in short supply under the impact of fossil fuels. The next decades will reveal the outcome of this titanic struggle and thereby resolve the question whether or not our industrial civilization has a future.

The vision of the hydrogen economy outlined a half-century ago by John O'Malley Bockris is at last coming to fruition. The politics of the energy transition has reached the point where the proponents of green hydrogen and renewable energy are starting to outweigh the defenders of the fossil fuels status quo, in terms not just of policies but of weight of investment and economic interests. Bockris would no doubt be delighted to see such a powerful vindication of his work, in framing a strategy for survival on the part of our industrial civilization.

BIBLIOGRAPHY

Altenburg, Tilman, Albaledejo, Manuel, Fokeer, Smeeta, and Wenck, Nele 2022. Green hydrogen. Opportunities for industrial development through forward linkages from renewables. Chapter "New research insights" in Sustainable Global Supply Chains report 2022, German Development Institute (DIE), at: https://www.idos-research.de /fileadmin/user_upload/pdfs/projekt/20220407_SustainableGlobalSupplyChains -Report2022_lowres.pdf

Alverà, Marco 2021. *The Hydrogen Revolution: A Blueprint for the Future of Clean Energy*. London: Hodder Studio.

Antal, M. and Van Den Bergh, J.C.J.M. 2014. Green growth and climate change: Conceptual and empirical considerations. *Climate Policy*, 16 (2): 165–177.

Bockris, John O'M. 1972. A hydrogen economy. *Science*, 176 (4041): 1323.

Bockris, John O'M. 1975. *Energy: The Solar-Hydrogen Alternative*. Sydney: Australia and New Zealand Book Company.

Bockris, John O'M. 2013. The hydrogen economy: Its history. *International Journal of Hydrogen Energy*, 38: 2579–2588.

Bockris, John O'M. and Veziroglu, T. Nejat 1985. A solar-hydrogen energy system for environmental compatibility. *Environmental Conservation*, 12 (2): 105–118.

Breyer, Christian, Khalili, S., Bogdanov, D., Ram, M., Oyewo, A.S., Aghahosseini, A., Gulagi, A., Solomon, A.A., Keiner, D., Lopez, G., Ostergard, P.A., Lund, H., Mathiesen, B.V., Jacobson, M.Z., Victoria, M., Teske, S., Pregger, T., Fthenakis, V., Raugei, M., Holttinen, H., Bardi, U., Hoekstra, A., and Sovacool, B.K. 2022. On the history and future of 100% renewable energy systems research. *IEEE Access*, 10: 78176.

Collier, Paul and Venables, A.J. 2012. Greening Africa? Constraints, technologies, and comparative costs. *Energy Economics*, 34 (Suppl. 1): S75–S84.

Conte, M., Iacobuzzi, A., Ronchetti, M. and Vellone, R. 2001. Hydrogen economy for a sustainable development: State-of-the-art and technological perspectives. *Journal of Power Sources*, 100: 171–187.

Daiyan, Rahman, Macgill, Iain and Amal, Rose 2020. Opportunities and challenges for renewable power-to-X. *ACS Energy Letters*, 5 (12): 3843–3847.

Daly, Herman E. 1974. Steady state economics vs growth mania: A critique of the orthodox conceptions of growth, wants, scarcity and efficiency. *Policy Science*, 5 (2): 149–167.

Eljack, Fadwa and Kazi, Monzure-Khoda 2021. Prospects and challenges of green hydrogen economy in multi-sector global symbiosis in Qatar. *Frontiers in Sustainability*, 1: 612762: https://www.frontiersin.org/articles/10.3389/frsus.2020.612762/full

Fagerberg, Jan 2022. Mobilizing innovation for sustainability transitions: A comment on transformative innovation policy. *Research Policy* (forthcoming), available at: https://www.sciencedirect.com/science/article/pii/S0048733318301999

Garnaut, Ross 2019. *Superpower: Australia's Low Carbon Opportunity*. Melbourne: Black Inc.

Guo, J., Zhang, Y., Zawabeti, A., Chen, K., Guo, Y., Fan, X., and Gang, L. 2022. Hydrogen production from the air. *Nature Communications*, 13 (1–9): 5046.

Haldane, J.B.S. 1923. *Daedalus, or Science and the Future*. Cambridge Heretics, available at: https://archive.org/details/daedalus_or_science_and_the_future

Hodges, A., Hoang, A.L., Tsekouras, G., Wagner, K., Lee, C.Y., Swiegers, E.F. and Wallace, G.G. 2022. A high-performance capillary-fed electrolysis cell promises more cost-competitive renewable hydrogen. *Nature Communications*. https://www.nature.com/articles/s41467-022-28953-x.pdf

IEA 2019. *The Future of Hydrogen*. Paris: International Energy Agency. https://www.iea.org/reports/the-future-of-hydrogen

IEA 2021. *World Energy Balances*. Paris: International Energy Agency.

IRENA 2020. *Green Hydrogen Cost Reduction: Scaling up Electrolysers to Meet the 1.5 Climate Goal*. Abu Dhabi: International Renewable Energy Agency. https://irena.org/-/media/Files/IRENA/Agency/Publication/2020/Dec/IRENA_Green_hydrogen_cost_2020.pdf

Jackson, Tim 2009. *Prosperity Without Growth: Economics for a Finite Planet*. London: Earthscan.

Jones, Eric L. 1988. *Growth Recurring: Economic Change in World History*. Oxford, UK: Clarendon Press.

Kaldor, Nicholas 1970. The case for regional policies. *Scottish Journal of Political Economy*, 17: 337–348.

Lamy, Claude and Millet, Pierre 2020. A critical review on the definitions used to calculate the energy efficiency coefficients of water electrolysis cells working under near ambient temperature conditions. *Journal of Power Engineering*, 447: 227350, at: https://www.sciencedirect.com/science/article/abs/pii/S0378775319313436

Lebrouhi, B.E., Djoupo, J.J., Lamrani, B., Benabdelaziz, K. and Kousksou, T. 2022. Global hydrogen development: A technological and geopolitical overview. *International Journal of Hydrogen Energy*, 47: 7016–7048.

Lee, Keun 2021. *China's Technological Leapfrogging and Economic Catch-Up: A Schumpeterian Perspective*. Oxford, UK: Oxford University Press.

Leggett, Jeremy 2018. *The Winning of the Carbon War: Power and Politics on the Front Lines of Climate and Clean Energy*. London: Crux Publishing.

Mathews, John A. 2011. Naturalizing capitalism: The next great transformation. *Futures*, 43: 868–879.

Mathews, John A. 2013. The renewable energies technology surge: A new techno-economic paradigm in the making? *Futures*, 46: 10–22.

Mathews, John A. 2015. *Greening of Capitalism: How Asia is Driving the Next Great Transformation*. Redwood, CA: Stanford University Press.

Mathews, John A. 2016a. Latecomer industrialization. Chapter 32 in Erik S. Reinert, Jayati Ghosh and Rainer Kattel (eds), *Handbook of Alternative Theories of Economic Development*, pp. 613–636. Edward Elgar Publishing.

Mathews, John A. 2016b. Global trade and promotion of cleantech industry: A post-Paris agenda. *Climate Policy*, 17 (1): 102–110.

Mathews, John A. 2017. *Global Green Shift: When CERES Meets GAIA*. London: Anthem Press.

Mathews, John A. 2019. The green growth economy as an engine of development: The case of China. Chapter 14 in R. Fouquet (ed), *Handbook on Green Growth*. Cheltenham, UK: Edward Elgar.

Mathews, John A. 2020. The greening of industrial hubs. Chapter 24 in Arkebe Oqubay and Justin Yifu Lin (eds), *The Oxford Handbook of Industrial Hubs and Economic Development*. Oxford, UK: OUP.

Mathews, John A. 2021. Schumpeterian economic dynamics of greening: Propagation of green eco-platforms. Chapter 14 in A. Pyka and K. Lee (eds), *Innovation, Catch-up and Sustainable Development: A Schumpeterian Perspective*. Cham, Switzerland: Springer.

Mathews, John A. and Cho, Dong-Sung 2000. *Tiger Technology: The Creation of a Semiconductor Industry in East Asia*. Cambridge: Cambridge University Press.

Mathews, John A. and Kidney, S. 2012. Financing climate-friendly energy development through bonds, *Development Southern Africa*, 29 (2): 337–349.

Mathews, John A. and Reinert, Erik S. 2014. Renewables, manufacturing and green growth: Energy strategies based on capturing increasing returns. *Futures* (Sep), 61: 13–22.

Mathews, John A. and Tan, Hao 2014. Manufacture renewables to build energy security. *Nature*, 513 (11 September): 166–168.

Mathews, John A. and Tan, Hao 2016. Circular economy: Lessons from China. *Nature*, 331 (24 March): 440–442.

Murphy, K.M., Schleifer, A. and Vishny, R.W. 1989. Industrialization and the big push. *Journal of Political Economy*, 97 (5): 1003–1026.

Myrdal, Gunnar 1957. *Economic Theory and Under-developed Regions*. London: Duckworth.

Nordhaus, William D. 2021. *The Spirit of Green: The Economics of Collisions and Contagions in a Crowded World*. Princeton, NJ: Princeton University Press.

Obodo, Kingsley Onyebuchi, Ouma, Cecil Naphtaly Moro, and Bessarabov, Dmitri 2021. Low-temperature water electrolysis. Chapter 2 in G. Spazzafumo (ed), *Power to Fuel: How to Speed Up a Hydrogen Economy*, pp. 17–50. Cambridge, MA: Academic Press.

OECD 2011. *Towards Green Growth*. Paris: OECD Publishing.

Oliveira, Alexandra M., Beswick, Rebecca R. and Yan, Yushan 2021. A green hydrogen economy for a renewable energy society. *Current Opinions in Chemical Engineering*, 33: 100701. https://www.sciencedirect.com/science/article/abs/pii/S2211339821000332

Perez, Carlota 2016. Capitalism, technology and a green global golden age: The role of history in helping to shape the future. Chapter 11 in M. Mazzucato and M. Jacobs (eds), *Rethinking Capitalism*, pp. 191–217. London: Wiley Blackwell.

Perez, Carlota and Murray-Leach, Tamsin 2021. Beyond 4.0. technological revolutions: Which ones, how many and why it matters – a neo-Schumpeterian view. Historical background paper WP7-D7.1. London: UCL, Institute for Innovation and Public Purpose, at: https://www.beyond4-0.eu/

Phoumin, Han 2021. The role of hydrogen in ASEAN's clean energy future. National Bureau of Asian Research. Available at: https://www.nbr.org/publication/the-role-of-hydrogen-in-aseans-clean-energy-future/

Pyka, Andreas and Lee, Keun (eds) 2021. *Innovation, Catch-Up and Sustainable Development*. Cham, Switzerland: Springer.

Reinert, Erik S. 2016. Antonio Serra and the problems of today. Chapter 3 in Rosario Patalano and Sophus A. Reinert (eds), *Antonio Serra and the Economics of Good Government*, pp. 325–361. Springer.

Rifkin, Jeremy 2002. *The Hydrogen Economy: The Creation of the Worldwide Energy Web and the Redistribution of Power on Earth.* New York, NY: Jeremy Tarcher Perigee.

Romm, Joseph J. 2004. *The Hype About Hydrogen: Fact and Fiction in the Race to Save the Climate.* Washington, DC: Island Press.

Salmon, N. and Banares-Alcantara, R. 2021. Green ammonia as a spatial energy vector: A review. *Sustainable Energy & Fuels*, 5: 2814–2839.

Scheer, Hermann 2011. *The Energy Imperative: 100 Percent Renewable Now.* Abingdon, UK: Earthscan.

Schmalensee, R. 2012. From "green growth" to sound policies: An overview. *Energy Economics*, 34 (Suppl. 1): S2–S6.

Schot, Johan and Steinmueller, W. Edward 2018. Three frames for innovation policy: R&D, systems of innovation and transformative change. *Research Policy*, 47 (9): 1554–1567.

Schumpeter, Joseph A. 1942/1947. *Capitalism, Socialism, and Democracy.* New York: Harper Brothers.

Smil, Vaclav 2004. *Enriching the Earth: Fritz Haber, Carl Bosch, and the Transformation of World Food Production.* Cambridge, MA: MIT Press.

Spazzafumo, Giuseppe (ed) 2021. *Power to Fuel: How to Speed up a Hydrogen Economy.* Cambridge, MA: Academic Press.

Stangarone, Troy 2021. South Korean efforts to transition to a hydrogen economy. *Clean Technologies and Environmental Policy*, 23: 509–516.

Thompson, Helen 2021. *Disorder: Hard Times in the Twenty First Century.* Oxford: Oxford University Press.

Thompson, Helen 2022. The geopolitics of fossil fuels and renewables reshape the world. *Nature* (World view) (11 March 2022), 603: 364, at: https://www.nature.com/

Thurbon, Elizabeth, Kim, Sung-Young, Tan, Hao and Mathews, John A. 2023. *Developmental Environmentalism: State Ambition and Creative Destruction in East Asia's Green Energy Transition.* Oxford: Oxford University Press (forthcoming).

Young, Allyn 1928. Increasing returns and economic progress. *The Economic Journal*, 38 (152): 527–542.

Zeng, X., Mathews, J.A. and Li, Jinhui 2018. Urban mining of e-waste is becoming more cost-effective than virgin mining. *Environmental Science and Technology*, 52 (8): 4835–4841.

Ziegler, Micah S. and Trancik, Jessika A. 2021. Re-examining rates of lithium-ion battery technology improvement and cost decline. *Energy & Environmental Science*, 14: 1635–1651.

INDEX

CPSIA information can be obtained
at www.ICGtesting.com
Printed in the USA
BVHW030319220123
656826BV00001B/5